3rd Grade Math Workbook

Jungle Publishing

Introduction

This is a math book suitable for 8 - 9 year olds (Grade 3) looking to test out their math skills.

It can also be used by Grade 2 students wanting to get ahead and Grade 4 kids who want to maintain and refresh their knowledge.

The book is divided up into seven parts:

- Number and Place Value
- Addition and Subtraction
- Multiplication and Division
- Fractions
- Measurement
- Geometry
- Statistics

Some of the exercises are explained in more detail on page 5.

Answers are included at the back.

Good luck!

This book belongs to:

....

Table of Contents

Exercises Explained

Part-whole Models

Part-whole models require you to add the two 'part' numbers at the bottom to make the 'whole' number at the top. In the example the two parts, 7 + 4, would make the whole number of 11.

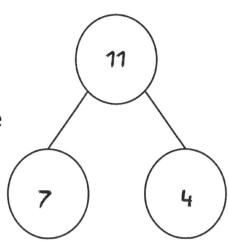

Fact Families

Fact families are groups of facts containing the same numbers.

Either two addition and two subtraction problems or two multiplication and two division problems will be given.

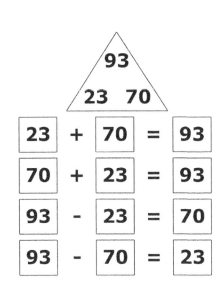

Bullseye

The bullseye drill requires you to multiply the central number by the numbers on the inner ring.

Enter the answer on the outer ring.

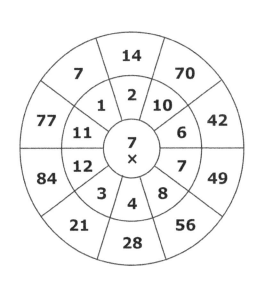

Section 1: Numbers and Place Value

Name: _____   Date: _____

Class: _____   Teacher: _____

Counting on a Line

Add the four numbers to the correct places on the line.

30, 70, 10, 75

30, 15, 60, 55

5, 95, 75, 55

20, 60, 35, 55

25, 55, 10, 35

35, 65, 30, 85

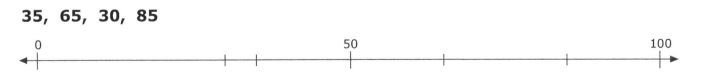

Add the four numbers to the correct places on the line.

27, 147, 127, 67

372, 412, 282, 452

451, 281, 381, 401

882, 902, 812, 792

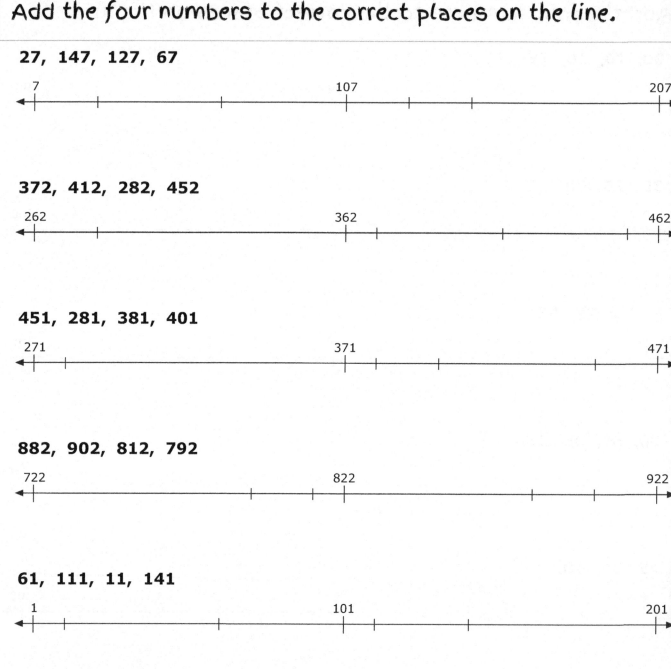

61, 111, 11, 141

798, 638, 748, 688

Before and After

Add the numbers that come before and after those below.

Example: 176... 177... 178

1) .... **414** ....

2) .... **598** ....

3) .... **352** ....

4) .... **524** ....

5) .... **306** ....

6) .... **332** ....

7) .... **896** ....

8) .... **632** ....

9) .... **769** ....

10) .... **663** ....

11) .... **576** ....

12) .... **649** ....

13) .... **780** ....

14) .... **735** ....

15) .... **682** ....

Circle the Smallest Numbers

1)	2)	3)	4)	5)
775	649	227	538	975
684	104	810	29	778
382	301	528	753	6
344	794	657	42	971
33	983	516	23	575

6)	7)	8)	9)	10)
427	717	849	586	915
271	895	799	476	219
886	4	930	211	510
983	464	985	29	58
858	942	383	705	709

Score: _____ /25

Circle the Biggest Numbers

1)	2)	3)	4)	5)
193	997	378	332	739
675	677	218	806	99
492	411	318	64	767
892	769	936	714	658
25	605	266	666	437

6)	7)	8)	9)	10)
498	207	41	172	368
566	760	402	388	158
977	827	112	161	275
265	273	438	380	762
659	664	945	5	373

Circle the Smallest and Biggest Numbers

1)	2)	3)	4)	5)
109	94	430	617	929
155	907	699	390	693
795	833	145	45	625
392	455	109	271	769
970	527	398	224	493

6)	7)	8)	9)	10)
350	340	51	133	472
937	291	965	569	242
387	215	435	657	51
653	891	302	911	981
68	550	570	514	387

Score: /20

Circle the Odd Numbers

1)	2)	3)	4)	5)
67	99	83	817	657
808	432	63	668	507
818	546	114	962	679
705	248	657	237	789
809	896	359	3	527

6)	7)	8)	9)	10)
849	907	31	117	722
121	776	451	662	34
8	617	626	702	390
699	543	699	633	838
575	306	949	33	256

Circle the Even Numbers

1)	2)	3)	4)	5)
97	738	210	553	313
268	824	974	866	998
638	323	103	458	169
319	725	761	209	206
283	773	285	906	773

6)	7)	8)	9)	10)
35	115	48	116	73
841	850	550	785	460
740	157	209	148	934
259	435	951	48	964
610	799	530	197	641

Score: /20

Numbers as words

Write these numbers as words.

1) **93**

2) **60**

3) **51**

4) **59**

5) **45**

6) **94**

7) **100**

8) **34**

9) **58**

10) **68**

Score: /10

Words as Numbers

Write these words as numbers.

1) **sixty-eight**

2) **forty-seven**

3) **nineteen**

4) **fifty-one**

5) **ninety-nine**

6) **eighty-eight**

7) **seventy-three**

8) **sixty**

9) **seventy-one**

10) **thirty-four**

Score: /10

Place Values

Determine the place value of the underlined digit. For example: '3 ones', or '6 tens'.

1) **99_2_** = ...

2) **7_8_** = ...

3) **80_7_** = ...

4) **_9_11** = ...

5) **40_6_** = ...

6) **3_1_0** = ...

7) **23_5_** = ...

8) **1_1_3** = ...

9) **_9_06** = ...

10) **_2_70** = ...

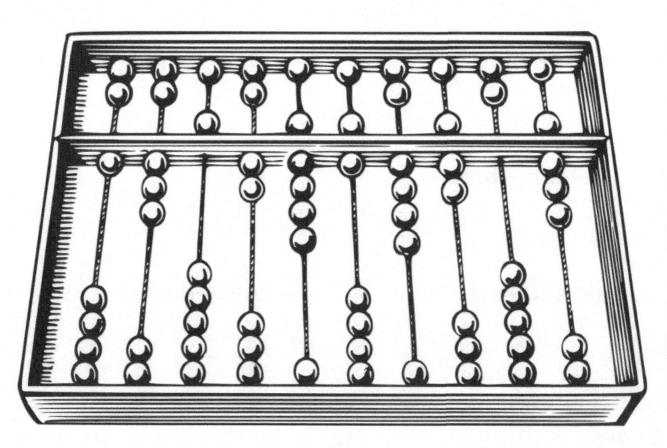

Number Comparison

Add > or < or =; Greater, less than or equal to (0-1000).

1) 1 350

2) 136 651

3) 248 359

4) 826 536

5) 542 460

6) 692 271

7) 137 335

8) 972 517

9) 567 500

10) 285 508

11) 234 922

12) 183 88

13) 906 49

14) 440 939

15) 941 70

Order the Numbers

Order each set from lowest to highest (smallest number to biggest number).

1) 177 ....
    246 ....
    892 ....
    504 ....
    439 ....
     44 ....

2) 481 ....
    957 ....
    210 ....
    619 ....
    553 ....
     68 ....

3) 248 ....
    717 ....
    674 ....
    651 ....
    420 ....
    676 ....

Fill in the Missing Numbers

1)

	50				70	75			90
45	50	55	60	65	70	75	80	85	90

2)

104	112				144				176
104	112	120	128	136	144	152	160	168	176

3)

50	60							130	140
50	60	70	80	90	100	110	120	130	140

4)

160		152					132	128	
160	156	152	148	144	140	136	132	128	124

5)

		200	250		350	400			
100	150	200	250	300	350	400	450	500	550

6)

	200	300				700	800		
100	200	300	400	500	600	700	800	900	1000

7)

600	550				350				150
600	550	500	450	400	350	300	250	200	150

8)

				68			56	52	48
84	80	76	72	68	64	60	56	52	48

9)

450	500	550	600						
450	500	550	600	650	700	750	800	850	900

10)

	730			690			660		
740	730	720	710	700	690	680	670	660	650

Section 2: Addition and Subtraction

Name: _____   Date: _____

Class: _____   Teacher: _____

Add these objects together. Draw them on!

1) 🍎🍎🍎🍎🍎 🍎🍎🍎🍎🍎 🍎🍎🍎 + 🍎🍎🍎🍎🍎 🍎🍎🍎🍎🍎 🍎🍎🍎🍎 🍎🍎 =

2) ⭐⭐⭐⭐⭐ ⭐⭐⭐⭐⭐ ⭐ + ⭐⭐⭐⭐⭐ ⭐⭐⭐⭐⭐ ⭐⭐⭐⭐⭐ ⭐ =

3) ❤❤❤❤❤ ❤❤❤❤❤ ❤❤❤❤ ❤ + ❤❤❤❤❤ ❤❤❤❤ ❤❤❤❤ =

Score: /3

Part-Whole Models

Fill out these part-whole models.

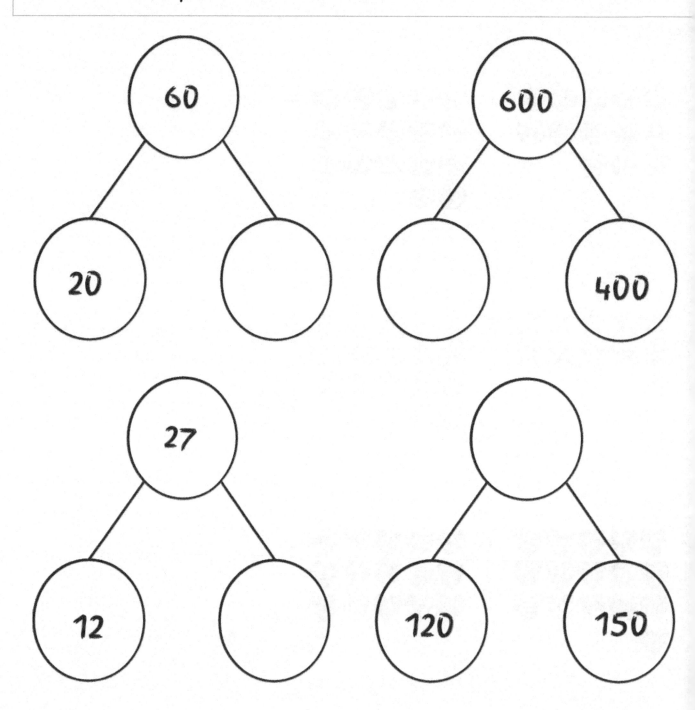

Adding Toucans

How many toucans can you see here?

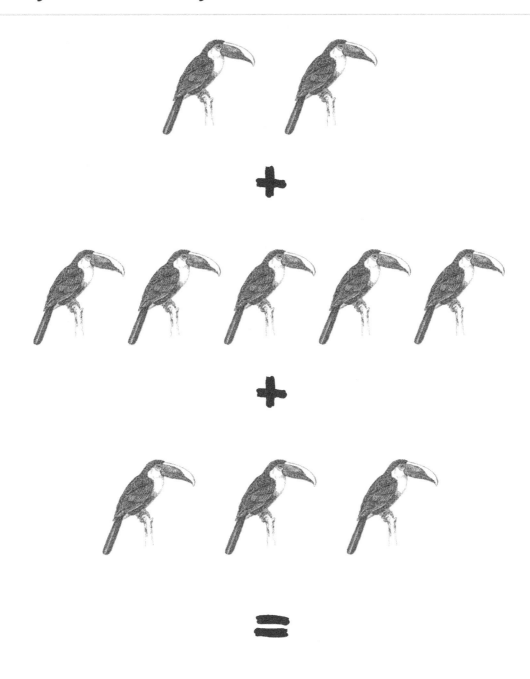

....

1)
```
     8
    22
 + 24
```

2)
```
    23
    11
 + 11
```

3)
```
    18
     3
 +   9
```

4)
```
     8
    18
 +   9
```

5)
```
    25
    26
 + 25
```

6)
```
     9
    21
 + 22
```

7)
```
    24
    23
 +   7
```

8)
```
    28
    16
 + 17
```

9)
```
     5
    22
 +   9
```

10)
```
     4
     6
 + 27
```

11)
```
     3
    19
 + 20
```

12)
```
    17
     1
 + 24
```

13)
```
    23
    27
 + 10
```

14)
```
    21
    18
 +   7
```

15)
```
    18
     8
 + 25
```

Score: _____ /15

Fact Families: Addition and Subtraction

Complete these addition and subtraction families.

1)

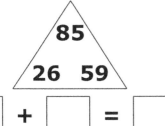

85

26   59

☐ + ☐ = ☐

☐ + ☐ = ☐

☐ - ☐ = ☐

☐ - ☐ = ☐

2)

73

56   17

☐ + ☐ = ☐

☐ + ☐ = ☐

☐ - ☐ = ☐

☐ - ☐ = ☐

3)

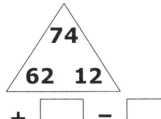

74

62   12

☐ + ☐ = ☐

☐ + ☐ = ☐

☐ - ☐ = ☐

☐ - ☐ = ☐

4)

94

65   29

☐ + ☐ = ☐

☐ + ☐ = ☐

☐ - ☐ = ☐

☐ - ☐ = ☐

Score: /4

Written Questions

Solve these written questions.

a) What is 760 + 10?

_____

b) What does 14 tens + 3 ones equal?

_____

c) 120 - 12 + 10?

_____

d) What is the sum of 201 + 20?

_____

e) What number is halfway between 320 and 360?

_____

f) 131 - 15?

_____

Complete this counting table. Go from left to right.

1) **Count by 5 from 5 to 240**

5				
		45		
65		75		90
		140	145	
	220	225		240

1) **68 + 14 =** _____

2) **25 - 5 =** _____

3) **61 + 10 =** _____

4) **54 - 10 =** _____

5) **35 + 12 =** _____

6) **61 + 15 =** _____

7) **52 - 9 =** _____

8) **99 - 84 =** _____

9) **72 - 41 =** _____

10) **59 + 24 =** _____

11) **47 - 31 =** _____

12) **96 - 19 =** _____

13) **33 - 8 =** _____

14) **15 + 18 =** _____

15) **38 - 17 =** _____

16) **45 - 25 =** _____

17) **13 + 12 =** _____

18) **48 + 42 =** _____

19) **24 + 28 =** _____

20) **14 + 24 =** _____

Score: /20

Mixed Operations 0-100: Part 2

1)   27
   + 46

2)   61
   + 37

3)   20
   - 10

4)   16
   - 11

5)   13
   - 11

6)   27
   + 54

7)   16
   - 12

8)   55
   + 44

9)   43
   + 46

10)   13
   - 13

11)   17
   - 16

12)   25
   + 68

13)   11
   - 10

14)   18
   - 17

15)   26
   + 57

16)   52
   + 35

17)   12
   - 10

18)   49
   + 22

19)   19
   - 11

20)   15
   - 10

21)   17
   - 10

22)   31
   + 66

23)   33
   + 66

24)   17
   - 15

25)   17
   - 14

26)   18
   - 14

27)   49
   + 31

28)   55
   + 43

29)   40
   + 54

30)   51
   + 30

Score: /30

Charlie Croc!

Total the numbers from Charlie Crocodile's balloons.

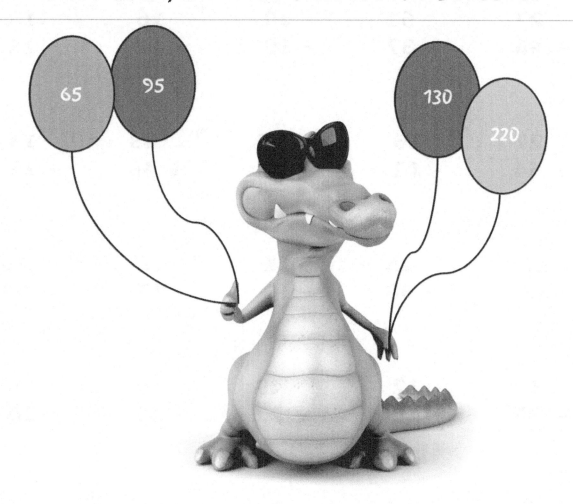

Left-hand side: **Right-hand side:**

_____   _____

Oops, the balloon on the far left and far right have burst! Add the remaining two numbers.

_____

Adding Numbers 0-1000: Part 1

Adding a multiple of 10 to a three-digit number.

1)
```
   260
+   10
------
```

2)
```
   482
+   10
------
```

3)
```
   414
+   30
------
```

4)
```
   122
+   50
------
```

5)
```
   224
+   10
------
```

6)
```
   297
+   20
------
```

7)
```
   481
+   50
------
```

8)
```
   264
+   40
------
```

9)
```
   391
+   10
------
```

10)
```
   222
+   50
------
```

11)
```
   384
+   60
------
```

12)
```
   461
+   30
------
```

13)
```
   216
+   60
------
```

14)
```
   500
+   10
------
```

15)
```
   490
+   10
------
```

16)
```
   207
+   50
------
```

17)
```
   168
+   70
------
```

18)
```
   198
+   20
------
```

19)
```
   407
+   70
------
```

20)
```
   298
+   40
------
```

Score: _____ /20

Adding Numbers 0-1000: Part 2

Adding a multiple of 100 to a three-digit number.

1) 192 + 100

2) 464 + 400

3) 450 + 300

4) 204 + 500

5) 417 + 100

6) 204 + 500

7) 387 + 400

8) 284 + 400

9) 257 + 100

10) 128 + 200

11) 160 + 200

12) 307 + 300

13) 303 + 100

14) 446 + 400

15) 329 + 400

16) 188 + 400

17) 282 + 200

18) 400 + 400

19) 384 + 500

20) 256 + 500

Score: /20

Subtracting Numbers 0-1000: Part 1

Subtracting a multiple of 10 from a three-digit number.

1) $\begin{array}{r} 252 \\ -40 \\ \hline \end{array}$
2) $\begin{array}{r} 619 \\ -60 \\ \hline \end{array}$
3) $\begin{array}{r} 238 \\ -30 \\ \hline \end{array}$
4) $\begin{array}{r} 288 \\ -30 \\ \hline \end{array}$
5) $\begin{array}{r} 126 \\ -60 \\ \hline \end{array}$

6) $\begin{array}{r} 571 \\ -30 \\ \hline \end{array}$
7) $\begin{array}{r} 306 \\ -70 \\ \hline \end{array}$
8) $\begin{array}{r} 308 \\ -40 \\ \hline \end{array}$
9) $\begin{array}{r} 306 \\ -70 \\ \hline \end{array}$
10) $\begin{array}{r} 432 \\ -60 \\ \hline \end{array}$

11) $\begin{array}{r} 640 \\ -10 \\ \hline \end{array}$
12) $\begin{array}{r} 812 \\ -60 \\ \hline \end{array}$
13) $\begin{array}{r} 560 \\ -10 \\ \hline \end{array}$
14) $\begin{array}{r} 428 \\ -70 \\ \hline \end{array}$
15) $\begin{array}{r} 207 \\ -70 \\ \hline \end{array}$

16) $\begin{array}{r} 457 \\ -70 \\ \hline \end{array}$
17) $\begin{array}{r} 347 \\ -10 \\ \hline \end{array}$
18) $\begin{array}{r} 477 \\ -70 \\ \hline \end{array}$
19) $\begin{array}{r} 603 \\ -40 \\ \hline \end{array}$
20) $\begin{array}{r} 456 \\ -50 \\ \hline \end{array}$

Score: _____ /20

Subtracting a multiple of 100 from a three-digit number.

1) 595 − 100

2) 287 − 100

3) 817 − 700

4) 531 − 300

5) 873 − 200

6) 780 − 500

7) 849 − 700

8) 331 − 100

9) 851 − 300

10) 680 − 500

11) 599 − 400

12) 649 − 400

13) 872 − 700

14) 341 − 100

15) 836 − 100

16) 771 − 500

17) 691 − 400

18) 668 − 200

19) 493 − 100

20) 599 − 400

Score: /20

Mixed Operations 0-1000

1) $382 + 190$

2) $613 - 257$

3) $499 + 259$

4) $465 - 254$

5) $238 + 127$

6) $252 + 701$

7) $579 + 401$

8) $650 - 311$

9) $760 - 272$

10) $208 + 331$

11) $448 - 297$

12) $328 - 177$

13) $646 + 208$

14) $965 - 141$

15) $746 - 469$

16) $301 + 409$

17) $550 - 178$

18) $646 - 185$

19) $206 + 198$

20) $154 + 165$

21) $883 - 184$

22) $671 + 229$

23) $615 - 173$

24) $499 - 301$

25) $653 + 152$

26) $111 + 775$

27) $755 - 394$

28) $412 + 540$

29) $502 - 107$

30) $155 + 725$

Score: /30

33

Section 3: Multiplication and Division

Name: _____ Date: _____

Class: _____ Teacher: _____

Multiplying by 1-4: Part 1

1)   1   × 12

2)   3   × 12

3)   2   × 5

4)   2   × 10

5)   3   × 4

6)   3   × 11

7)   3   × 2

8)   1   × 11

9)   3   × 9

10)   4   × 11

11)   1   × 10

12)   4   × 7

13)   2   × 4

14)   4   × 10

15)   2   × 3

16)   4   × 4

17)   2   × 11

18)   3   × 8

19)   2   × 8

20)   3   × 10

21)   1   × 4

22)   4   × 8

23)   3   × 5

24)   3   × 3

25)   4   × 9

26)   3   × 1

27)   2   × 12

28)   3   × 6

29)   3   × 7

30)   4   × 3

31)   2   × 2

32)   1   × 6

33)   1   × 8

34)   4   × 6

35)   2   × 9

36)   4   × 2

37)   4   × 5

38)   1   × 7

39)   2   × 7

40)   1   × 1

Score: /40

1) $\begin{array}{r} 5 \\ \times\ 3 \\ \hline \end{array}$
2) $\begin{array}{r} 4 \\ \times\ 2 \\ \hline \end{array}$
3) $\begin{array}{r} 8 \\ \times\ 2 \\ \hline \end{array}$
4) $\begin{array}{r} 11 \\ \times\ 4 \\ \hline \end{array}$
5) $\begin{array}{r} 2 \\ \times\ 4 \\ \hline \end{array}$

6) $\begin{array}{r} 9 \\ \times\ 2 \\ \hline \end{array}$
7) $\begin{array}{r} 6 \\ \times\ 2 \\ \hline \end{array}$
8) $\begin{array}{r} 7 \\ \times\ 1 \\ \hline \end{array}$
9) $\begin{array}{r} 10 \\ \times\ 4 \\ \hline \end{array}$
10) $\begin{array}{r} 2 \\ \times\ 2 \\ \hline \end{array}$

11) $\begin{array}{r} 1 \\ \times\ 3 \\ \hline \end{array}$
12) $\begin{array}{r} 4 \\ \times\ 3 \\ \hline \end{array}$
13) $\begin{array}{r} 12 \\ \times\ 2 \\ \hline \end{array}$
14) $\begin{array}{r} 7 \\ \times\ 4 \\ \hline \end{array}$
15) $\begin{array}{r} 3 \\ \times\ 3 \\ \hline \end{array}$

16) $\begin{array}{r} 10 \\ \times\ 1 \\ \hline \end{array}$
17) $\begin{array}{r} 8 \\ \times\ 4 \\ \hline \end{array}$
18) $\begin{array}{r} 5 \\ \times\ 1 \\ \hline \end{array}$
19) $\begin{array}{r} 7 \\ \times\ 2 \\ \hline \end{array}$
20) $\begin{array}{r} 10 \\ \times\ 2 \\ \hline \end{array}$

21) $\begin{array}{r} 8 \\ \times\ 3 \\ \hline \end{array}$
22) $\begin{array}{r} 1 \\ \times\ 4 \\ \hline \end{array}$
23) $\begin{array}{r} 8 \\ \times\ 1 \\ \hline \end{array}$
24) $\begin{array}{r} 5 \\ \times\ 2 \\ \hline \end{array}$
25) $\begin{array}{r} 12 \\ \times\ 4 \\ \hline \end{array}$

26) $\begin{array}{r} 3 \\ \times\ 2 \\ \hline \end{array}$
27) $\begin{array}{r} 9 \\ \times\ 4 \\ \hline \end{array}$
28) $\begin{array}{r} 2 \\ \times\ 3 \\ \hline \end{array}$
29) $\begin{array}{r} 9 \\ \times\ 3 \\ \hline \end{array}$
30) $\begin{array}{r} 7 \\ \times\ 3 \\ \hline \end{array}$

31) $\begin{array}{r} 11 \\ \times\ 3 \\ \hline \end{array}$
32) $\begin{array}{r} 2 \\ \times\ 1 \\ \hline \end{array}$
33) $\begin{array}{r} 9 \\ \times\ 1 \\ \hline \end{array}$
34) $\begin{array}{r} 10 \\ \times\ 3 \\ \hline \end{array}$
35) $\begin{array}{r} 11 \\ \times\ 2 \\ \hline \end{array}$

36) $\begin{array}{r} 3 \\ \times\ 4 \\ \hline \end{array}$
37) $\begin{array}{r} 6 \\ \times\ 4 \\ \hline \end{array}$
38) $\begin{array}{r} 6 \\ \times\ 3 \\ \hline \end{array}$
39) $\begin{array}{r} 12 \\ \times\ 3 \\ \hline \end{array}$
40) $\begin{array}{r} 5 \\ \times\ 4 \\ \hline \end{array}$

Score: /40

Which two pairs of numbers can be multiplied to make 12?

$\underline{} \times \underline{} = 12$

$\underline{} \times \underline{} = 12$

12

$\underline{} \times \underline{} = 12$

$\underline{} \times \underline{} = 12$

Multiplying by 5-8: Part 1

1) 7×10

2) 7×5

3) 7×11

4) 6×4

5) 6×3

6) 7×2

7) 5×5

8) 6×11

9) 6×8

10) 8×3

11) 6×10

12) 6×5

13) 5×4

14) 6×7

15) 8×11

16) 8×8

17) 8×10

18) 6×12

19) 8×9

20) 8×4

21) 8×12

22) 7×7

23) 7×4

24) 6×9

25) 7×12

26) 7×1

27) 5×10

28) 7×6

29) 6×6

30) 5×11

31) 7×8

32) 5×12

33) 6×2

34) 8×6

35) 6×1

36) 8×5

37) 5×7

38) 8×7

39) 5×1

40) 8×1

Score: /40

Multiplying by 5-8: Part 2

1) $\begin{array}{r} 2 \\ \times\ 6 \\ \hline \end{array}$ 2) $\begin{array}{r} 3 \\ \times\ 6 \\ \hline \end{array}$ 3) $\begin{array}{r} 6 \\ \times\ 7 \\ \hline \end{array}$ 4) $\begin{array}{r} 4 \\ \times\ 5 \\ \hline \end{array}$ 5) $\begin{array}{r} 1 \\ \times\ 5 \\ \hline \end{array}$

6) $\begin{array}{r} 9 \\ \times\ 8 \\ \hline \end{array}$ 7) $\begin{array}{r} 7 \\ \times\ 5 \\ \hline \end{array}$ 8) $\begin{array}{r} 3 \\ \times\ 7 \\ \hline \end{array}$ 9) $\begin{array}{r} 2 \\ \times\ 8 \\ \hline \end{array}$ 10) $\begin{array}{r} 4 \\ \times\ 8 \\ \hline \end{array}$

11) $\begin{array}{r} 11 \\ \times\ 6 \\ \hline \end{array}$ 12) $\begin{array}{r} 1 \\ \times\ 6 \\ \hline \end{array}$ 13) $\begin{array}{r} 7 \\ \times\ 7 \\ \hline \end{array}$ 14) $\begin{array}{r} 11 \\ \times\ 8 \\ \hline \end{array}$ 15) $\begin{array}{r} 11 \\ \times\ 7 \\ \hline \end{array}$

16) $\begin{array}{r} 6 \\ \times\ 5 \\ \hline \end{array}$ 17) $\begin{array}{r} 10 \\ \times\ 6 \\ \hline \end{array}$ 18) $\begin{array}{r} 12 \\ \times\ 7 \\ \hline \end{array}$ 19) $\begin{array}{r} 5 \\ \times\ 6 \\ \hline \end{array}$ 20) $\begin{array}{r} 9 \\ \times\ 7 \\ \hline \end{array}$

21) $\begin{array}{r} 2 \\ \times\ 5 \\ \hline \end{array}$ 22) $\begin{array}{r} 9 \\ \times\ 6 \\ \hline \end{array}$ 23) $\begin{array}{r} 8 \\ \times\ 8 \\ \hline \end{array}$ 24) $\begin{array}{r} 3 \\ \times\ 8 \\ \hline \end{array}$ 25) $\begin{array}{r} 6 \\ \times\ 6 \\ \hline \end{array}$

26) $\begin{array}{r} 1 \\ \times\ 8 \\ \hline \end{array}$ 27) $\begin{array}{r} 3 \\ \times\ 5 \\ \hline \end{array}$ 28) $\begin{array}{r} 7 \\ \times\ 6 \\ \hline \end{array}$ 29) $\begin{array}{r} 12 \\ \times\ 6 \\ \hline \end{array}$ 30) $\begin{array}{r} 10 \\ \times\ 7 \\ \hline \end{array}$

31) $\begin{array}{r} 8 \\ \times\ 7 \\ \hline \end{array}$ 32) $\begin{array}{r} 5 \\ \times\ 8 \\ \hline \end{array}$ 33) $\begin{array}{r} 4 \\ \times\ 7 \\ \hline \end{array}$ 34) $\begin{array}{r} 8 \\ \times\ 6 \\ \hline \end{array}$ 35) $\begin{array}{r} 7 \\ \times\ 8 \\ \hline \end{array}$

36) $\begin{array}{r} 9 \\ \times\ 5 \\ \hline \end{array}$ 37) $\begin{array}{r} 4 \\ \times\ 6 \\ \hline \end{array}$ 38) $\begin{array}{r} 2 \\ \times\ 7 \\ \hline \end{array}$ 39) $\begin{array}{r} 11 \\ \times\ 5 \\ \hline \end{array}$ 40) $\begin{array}{r} 8 \\ \times\ 5 \\ \hline \end{array}$

Score: _____ /40

1)

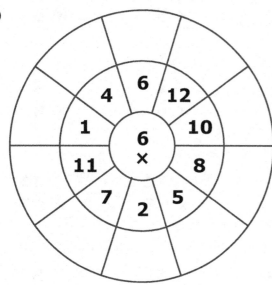

2)

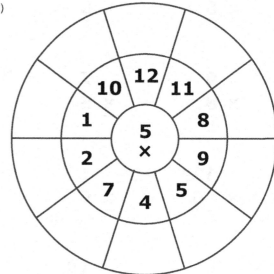

3)

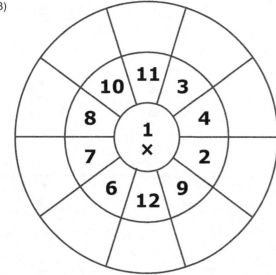

4)

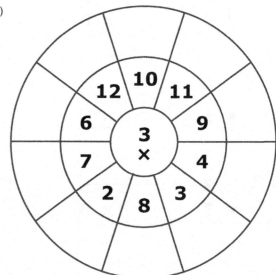

Score: /4

Multiplying by 9-12: Part 1

1) $\begin{array}{r} 11 \\ \times\ 12 \\ \hline \end{array}$
2) $\begin{array}{r} 11 \\ \times\ 8 \\ \hline \end{array}$
3) $\begin{array}{r} 10 \\ \times\ 2 \\ \hline \end{array}$
4) $\begin{array}{r} 10 \\ \times\ 7 \\ \hline \end{array}$
5) $\begin{array}{r} 11 \\ \times\ 7 \\ \hline \end{array}$

6) $\begin{array}{r} 10 \\ \times\ 11 \\ \hline \end{array}$
7) $\begin{array}{r} 12 \\ \times\ 5 \\ \hline \end{array}$
8) $\begin{array}{r} 9 \\ \times\ 7 \\ \hline \end{array}$
9) $\begin{array}{r} 9 \\ \times\ 6 \\ \hline \end{array}$
10) $\begin{array}{r} 11 \\ \times\ 4 \\ \hline \end{array}$

11) $\begin{array}{r} 10 \\ \times\ 10 \\ \hline \end{array}$
12) $\begin{array}{r} 10 \\ \times\ 12 \\ \hline \end{array}$
13) $\begin{array}{r} 11 \\ \times\ 2 \\ \hline \end{array}$
14) $\begin{array}{r} 9 \\ \times\ 3 \\ \hline \end{array}$
15) $\begin{array}{r} 10 \\ \times\ 6 \\ \hline \end{array}$

16) $\begin{array}{r} 11 \\ \times\ 11 \\ \hline \end{array}$
17) $\begin{array}{r} 12 \\ \times\ 6 \\ \hline \end{array}$
18) $\begin{array}{r} 11 \\ \times\ 5 \\ \hline \end{array}$
19) $\begin{array}{r} 10 \\ \times\ 9 \\ \hline \end{array}$
20) $\begin{array}{r} 10 \\ \times\ 5 \\ \hline \end{array}$

21) $\begin{array}{r} 12 \\ \times\ 4 \\ \hline \end{array}$
22) $\begin{array}{r} 11 \\ \times\ 1 \\ \hline \end{array}$
23) $\begin{array}{r} 12 \\ \times\ 8 \\ \hline \end{array}$
24) $\begin{array}{r} 9 \\ \times\ 11 \\ \hline \end{array}$
25) $\begin{array}{r} 9 \\ \times\ 10 \\ \hline \end{array}$

26) $\begin{array}{r} 12 \\ \times\ 12 \\ \hline \end{array}$
27) $\begin{array}{r} 9 \\ \times\ 12 \\ \hline \end{array}$
28) $\begin{array}{r} 12 \\ \times\ 11 \\ \hline \end{array}$
29) $\begin{array}{r} 11 \\ \times\ 6 \\ \hline \end{array}$
30) $\begin{array}{r} 11 \\ \times\ 10 \\ \hline \end{array}$

31) $\begin{array}{r} 12 \\ \times\ 10 \\ \hline \end{array}$
32) $\begin{array}{r} 12 \\ \times\ 3 \\ \hline \end{array}$
33) $\begin{array}{r} 11 \\ \times\ 9 \\ \hline \end{array}$
34) $\begin{array}{r} 10 \\ \times\ 1 \\ \hline \end{array}$
35) $\begin{array}{r} 12 \\ \times\ 1 \\ \hline \end{array}$

36) $\begin{array}{r} 11 \\ \times\ 3 \\ \hline \end{array}$
37) $\begin{array}{r} 9 \\ \times\ 2 \\ \hline \end{array}$
38) $\begin{array}{r} 10 \\ \times\ 4 \\ \hline \end{array}$
39) $\begin{array}{r} 9 \\ \times\ 5 \\ \hline \end{array}$
40) $\begin{array}{r} 12 \\ \times\ 7 \\ \hline \end{array}$

Score: _____ /40

Multiplying by 9-12: Part 2

1) 7 × 10

2) 9 × 10

3) 3 × 12

4) 5 × 12

5) 4 × 11

6) 11 × 10

7) 3 × 10

8) 5 × 10

9) 2 × 12

10) 7 × 11

11) 8 × 10

12) 10 × 11

13) 6 × 11

14) 8 × 12

15) 6 × 9

16) 2 × 11

17) 3 × 11

18) 10 × 12

19) 1 × 10

20) 9 × 9

21) 12 × 11

22) 1 × 11

23) 2 × 10

24) 8 × 11

25) 4 × 9

26) 12 × 10

27) 6 × 12

28) 6 × 10

29) 7 × 9

30) 4 × 12

31) 11 × 11

32) 11 × 12

33) 4 × 10

34) 10 × 10

35) 10 × 9

36) 7 × 12

37) 9 × 11

38) 11 × 9

39) 9 × 12

40) 5 × 11

Score: /40

Multiplication Word Problems

1) If there are three oranges in each box and there are eight boxes, how many oranges are there in total?

2) Jake swims two laps every day. How many laps will Jake swim in 10 days?

3) Alice's garden has two rows of pumpkins. Each row has eight pumpkins. How many pumpkins does Alice have in all?

4) David has six times more peaches than Adam. Adam has two peaches. How many peaches does David have?

5) David can cycle five miles per hour. How far can David cycle in eight hours?

Score: /5

43

Dividing by 1-5

1) $9 \div 1 =$ _____

2) $10 \div 5 =$ _____

3) $6 \div 3 =$ _____

4) $12 \div 4 =$ _____

5) $27 \div 3 =$ _____

6) $3 \div 1 =$ _____

7) $9 \div 3 =$ _____

8) $6 \div 1 =$ _____

9) $8 \div 4 =$ _____

10) $35 \div 5 =$ _____

11) $15 \div 3 =$ _____

12) $32 \div 4 =$ _____

13) $36 \div 4 =$ _____

14) $28 \div 4 =$ _____

15) $8 \div 1 =$ _____

16) $18 \div 2 =$ _____

17) $24 \div 4 =$ _____

18) $8 \div 2 =$ _____

19) $30 \div 3 =$ _____

20) $5 \div 1 =$ _____

Score: _____ /20

Dividing by 6-10

1) $64 \div 8 =$ _____

2) $56 \div 8 =$ _____

3) $9 \div 9 =$ _____

4) $14 \div 7 =$ _____

5) $36 \div 9 =$ _____

6) $72 \div 8 =$ _____

7) $40 \div 8 =$ _____

8) $80 \div 10 =$ _____

9) $81 \div 9 =$ _____

10) $16 \div 8 =$ _____

11) $32 \div 8 =$ _____

12) $35 \div 7 =$ _____

13) $60 \div 6 =$ _____

14) $48 \div 6 =$ _____

15) $12 \div 6 =$ _____

16) $49 \div 7 =$ _____

17) $90 \div 9 =$ _____

18) $60 \div 10 =$ _____

19) $72 \div 9 =$ _____

20) $63 \div 9 =$ _____

Score: _____ /20

Division Word Problems

1) Max is reading a book with 24 pages. If Max wants to read the same number of pages every day, how many pages would Max have to read each day to finish in three days?

2) You have 36 peaches and want to share them equally with four people. How many peaches would each person get?

3) Ellen made 45 cookies for a bake sale. She put the cookies in bags, with five cookies in each bag. How many bags did she have for the bake sale?

4) How many three cm pieces of rope can you cut from a rope that is 18 cm long?

5) Charlotte made 25 cookies for a bake sale. She put the cookies in bags, with five cookies in each bag. How many bags did she have for the bake sale?

Score: _____ /5

Fact Families: Multiplication and Division

Complete these fact families.

1)

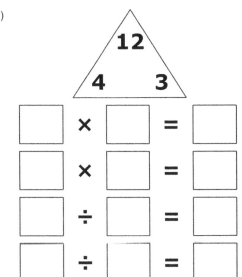

2)

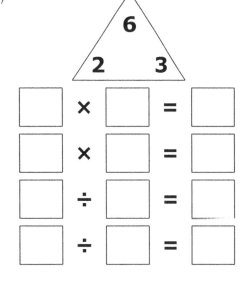

3)

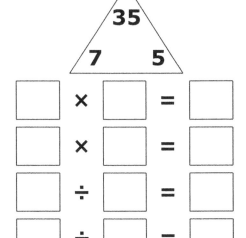

4)

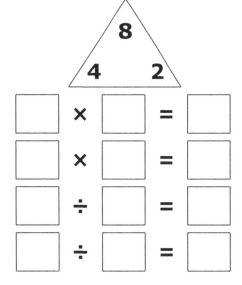

Score: ____ /4

The Maze!

Answer these sums and help Charlie through the maze!

10 x 3 =

26 ÷ 2 =

11 x 5 =

63 ÷ 7 =

8 x 9 =

5 x 6 =

7 x 5 =

5 x 9 =

Right or Wrong?

This table has 4 incorrect sums. Highlight the wrong ones!

2 x 1 = 2	32 ÷ 4 = 7	3 x 6 = 18
10 x 2 = 18	16 ÷ 5 = 4	4 x 5 = 20
100 ÷ 10 = 10	3 x 4 = 9	2 x 4 = 8
2 x 1 = 2	3 x 4 = 12	2 ÷ 2 = 1

Section 4: Fractions

Name: _____ Date: _____

Class: _____ Teacher: _____

Fill out the fractions for the shaded blocks below.

a) Which set of blocks represents a whole?

_____

b) Shade in a half of each of the blocks below. Choose a different method each time.

Shade the Fraction

Shade the rectangles as per the fraction provided.

1) $\dfrac{1}{3}$ =

2) $\dfrac{1}{8}$ =

3) $\dfrac{1}{2}$ =

4) $\dfrac{2}{3}$ =

5) $\dfrac{1}{5}$ =

6) $\dfrac{1}{4}$ =

7) $\dfrac{4}{6}$ =

8) $\dfrac{3}{8}$ =

9) $\dfrac{4}{5}$ =

10) $\dfrac{7}{8}$ =

Score: /10

Identify the Shaded Fraction

Identify the fraction as per the shaded rectangles.

1)  =

2)  =

3) 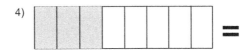 =

4) =

5) =

6) =

7) =

8) =

9) =

10) =

Score: /10

Charlie's Pizza

Draw a line to the fraction of the pizza Charlie has eaten.

$$\frac{1}{2} \qquad \frac{1}{3} \qquad \frac{1}{4} \qquad \frac{1}{5} \qquad \frac{2}{3} \qquad \frac{3}{4}$$

Charlie eats 1/2 of the remaining pizza. How much is left now?

Charlie is 16 miles from home...but he has his moped!

Charlie travels 4 miles. How much of his journey has he completed?

$$\frac{1}{2} \qquad \frac{1}{3} \qquad \frac{1}{4} \qquad \frac{1}{5} \qquad \frac{2}{3} \qquad \frac{3}{4}$$

He travels a further 10 miles. How much has he completed now?

$$\frac{1}{6} \qquad \frac{2}{3} \qquad \frac{5}{4} \qquad \frac{7}{8} \qquad \frac{2}{3} \qquad \frac{3}{6}$$

Fractions on a Line

Write the fraction in the appropriate place.

1)

$1\frac{1}{2}$ $\frac{1}{2}$ $\frac{3}{4}$ $1\frac{1}{4}$

2)

$1\frac{3}{4}$ $\frac{1}{4}$ $\frac{3}{4}$ $\frac{1}{2}$

3)

$\frac{1}{4}$ $1\frac{1}{4}$ $\frac{3}{4}$ $1\frac{3}{4}$

4)

$\frac{1}{4}$ $1\frac{3}{4}$ $\frac{3}{4}$ $1\frac{1}{4}$

Score: _____ /4

Add the Fractions

Find the sum of the two fractions.

1) $\dfrac{1}{10} + \dfrac{7}{10} =$

2) $\dfrac{2}{10} + \dfrac{1}{10} =$

3) $\dfrac{9}{10} + \dfrac{3}{10} =$

4) $\dfrac{8}{10} + \dfrac{3}{10} =$

5) $\dfrac{6}{10} + \dfrac{3}{10} =$

6) $\dfrac{5}{10} + \dfrac{7}{10} =$

7) $\dfrac{8}{10} + \dfrac{1}{10} =$

8) $\dfrac{1}{10} + \dfrac{1}{10} =$

9) $\dfrac{5}{10} + \dfrac{1}{10} =$

10) $\dfrac{9}{10} + \dfrac{9}{10} =$

Score: /10

Find the sum of the two fractions.

1) $+\dfrac{\frac{2}{4}}{\frac{3}{4}}$ 2) $+\dfrac{\frac{1}{3}}{\frac{2}{3}}$ 3) $+\dfrac{\frac{4}{5}}{\frac{4}{5}}$ 4) $+\dfrac{\frac{4}{6}}{\frac{1}{6}}$ 5) $+\dfrac{\frac{1}{2}}{\frac{1}{2}}$

6) $+\dfrac{\frac{2}{4}}{\frac{1}{4}}$ 7) $+\dfrac{\frac{2}{5}}{\frac{4}{5}}$ 8) $+\dfrac{\frac{2}{3}}{\frac{2}{3}}$ 9) $+\dfrac{\frac{1}{4}}{\frac{1}{4}}$ 10) $+\dfrac{\frac{2}{3}}{\frac{1}{3}}$

11) $+\dfrac{\frac{2}{5}}{\frac{3}{5}}$ 12) $+\dfrac{\frac{1}{6}}{\frac{1}{6}}$ 13) $+\dfrac{\frac{3}{4}}{\frac{1}{4}}$ 14) $+\dfrac{\frac{3}{6}}{\frac{1}{6}}$ 15) $+\dfrac{\frac{3}{5}}{\frac{4}{5}}$

16) $+\dfrac{\frac{3}{6}}{\frac{5}{6}}$ 17) $+\dfrac{\frac{2}{5}}{\frac{1}{5}}$ 18) $+\dfrac{\frac{4}{5}}{\frac{3}{5}}$ 19) $+\dfrac{\frac{5}{6}}{\frac{1}{6}}$ 20) $+\dfrac{\frac{1}{5}}{\frac{4}{5}}$

Score: /20

Group the Rhinos

A group of rhinos is called a 'crash'. There are 12 rhinos in this crash.

The crash splits into two equal groups.

a) There are now _____ sets of _____ rhinos.

b) How many ways could the two sets of rhinos be split further (into more equal groups)?

Simplifying Fractions

Simplify these fractions to their lowest common denominators.

1) $\dfrac{14}{28} =$

2) $\dfrac{12}{16} =$

3) $\dfrac{3}{9} =$

4) $\dfrac{2}{12} =$

5) $\dfrac{24}{48} =$

6) $\dfrac{10}{25} =$

7) $\dfrac{6}{8} =$

8) $\dfrac{2}{6} =$

9) $\dfrac{9}{15} =$

10) $\dfrac{27}{54} =$

11) $\dfrac{35}{40} =$

12) $\dfrac{40}{48} =$

13) $\dfrac{6}{12} =$

14) $\dfrac{18}{30} =$

15) $\dfrac{9}{24} =$

16) $\dfrac{12}{18} =$

17) $\dfrac{16}{48} =$

18) $\dfrac{5}{15} =$

19) $\dfrac{12}{48} =$

20) $\dfrac{4}{10} =$

Score: /20

Equivalent Fractions

Complete the equivalent fractions.

1) $\dfrac{2}{3} = \dfrac{}{24}$

2) $\dfrac{1}{4} = \dfrac{}{32}$

3) $\dfrac{1}{4} = \dfrac{}{40}$

4) $\dfrac{}{3} = \dfrac{8}{24}$

5) $\dfrac{1}{4} = \dfrac{}{24}$

6) $\dfrac{}{4} = \dfrac{10}{20}$

7) $\dfrac{1}{3} = \dfrac{}{30}$

8) $\dfrac{}{4} = \dfrac{9}{36}$

9) $\dfrac{}{3} = \dfrac{5}{15}$

10) $\dfrac{}{4} = \dfrac{6}{12}$

11) $\dfrac{}{3} = \dfrac{18}{27}$

12) $\dfrac{3}{4} = \dfrac{}{32}$

13) $\dfrac{1}{3} = \dfrac{}{21}$

14) $\dfrac{1}{3} = \dfrac{}{6}$

15) $\dfrac{}{3} = \dfrac{14}{21}$

16) $\dfrac{}{4} = \dfrac{12}{24}$

17) $\dfrac{2}{3} = \dfrac{}{18}$

18) $\dfrac{}{4} = \dfrac{16}{32}$

19) $\dfrac{1}{3} = \dfrac{}{9}$

20) $\dfrac{}{4} = \dfrac{21}{28}$

Score: /20

Comparing Fractions

Compare the numbers. Add: > or < or =

1) $\dfrac{3}{6}$ ___ $\dfrac{2}{4}$

2) $\dfrac{7}{8}$ ___ $\dfrac{1}{8}$

3) $\dfrac{3}{6}$ ___ $\dfrac{1}{4}$

4) $\dfrac{1}{3}$ ___ $\dfrac{2}{5}$

5) $\dfrac{1}{3}$ ___ $\dfrac{4}{6}$

6) $\dfrac{2}{5}$ ___ $\dfrac{3}{4}$

7) $\dfrac{7}{8}$ ___ $\dfrac{3}{4}$

8) $\dfrac{4}{6}$ ___ $\dfrac{7}{8}$

9) $\dfrac{3}{5}$ ___ $\dfrac{1}{4}$

10) $\dfrac{4}{6}$ ___ $\dfrac{1}{3}$

11) $\dfrac{5}{8}$ ___ $\dfrac{4}{5}$

12) $\dfrac{1}{8}$ ___ $\dfrac{1}{3}$

13) $\dfrac{3}{5}$ ___ $\dfrac{3}{4}$

14) $\dfrac{5}{6}$ ___ $\dfrac{2}{4}$

15) $\dfrac{5}{8}$ ___ $\dfrac{2}{3}$

16) $\dfrac{2}{5}$ ___ $\dfrac{5}{6}$

17) $\dfrac{4}{5}$ ___ $\dfrac{2}{3}$

18) $\dfrac{3}{4}$ ___ $\dfrac{7}{8}$

19) $\dfrac{4}{6}$ ___ $\dfrac{2}{4}$

20) $\dfrac{3}{6}$ ___ $\dfrac{2}{3}$

Score: _____ /20

Translating Fractions to Whole Numbers

Write in the numbers that are equal to these fractions.

1) $\frac{1}{3}$ of 6 =

2) $\frac{1}{5}$ of 5 =

3) $\frac{1}{6}$ of 6 =

4) $\frac{1}{4}$ of 8 =

5) $\frac{6}{8}$ of 8 =

6) $\frac{6}{10}$ of 10 =

7) $\frac{1}{2}$ of 4 =

8) $\frac{2}{3}$ of 3 =

9) $\frac{13}{20}$ of 20 =

10) $\frac{4}{6}$ of 6 =

11) $\frac{1}{2}$ of 6 =

12) $\frac{2}{5}$ of 5 =

13) $\frac{1}{4}$ of 4 =

14) $\frac{4}{8}$ of 8 =

15) $\frac{2}{10}$ of 10 =

16) $\frac{2}{3}$ of 6 =

17) $\frac{3}{20}$ of 20 =

18) $\frac{8}{10}$ of 10 =

19) $\frac{3}{6}$ of 6 =

20) $\frac{6}{20}$ of 20 =

Score: _____ /20

Shade the Fraction

Shade the blocks as per the fraction provided.

1) 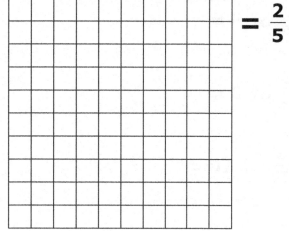 $= \dfrac{2}{5}$

2) 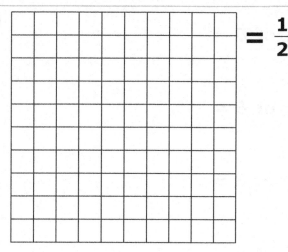 $= \dfrac{1}{2}$

3) 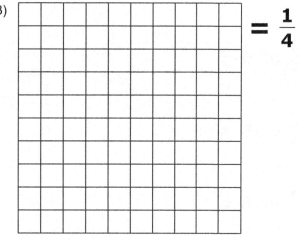 $= \dfrac{1}{4}$

4) 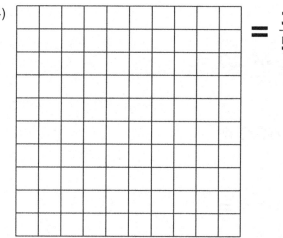 $= \dfrac{3}{5}$

5) 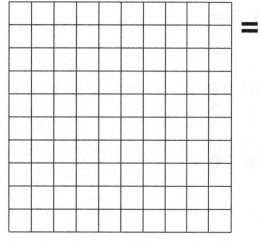 $= \dfrac{4}{5}$

6) 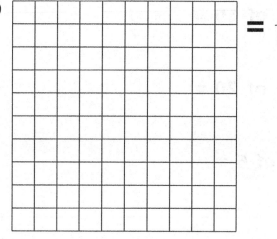 $= \dfrac{1}{5}$

Identify the Shaded Fraction

Write the fraction using the lowest common denominator.

1) 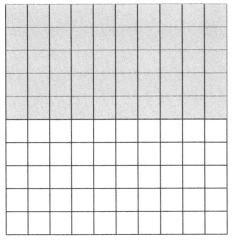 = _____

2) 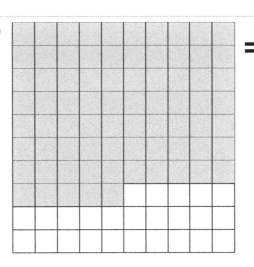 = _____

3) 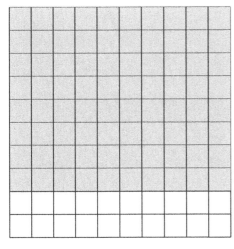 = _____

4) 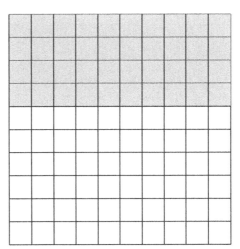 = _____

5) 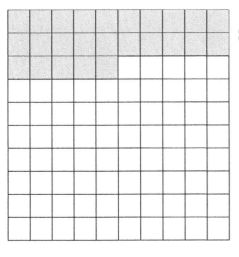 = _____

6) 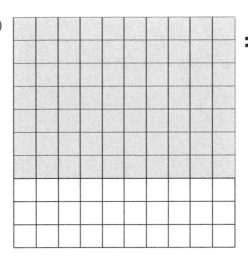 = _____

Section 5: Measurement

Name: _____ Date: _____

Class: _____ Teacher: _____

Measuring Lines

1)

_____

2)

_____

3)

_____

4)

_____

5)

_____

6)

_____

7)

_____

8)

_____

9)

_____

10)

_____

a) Measure the lines. Which line is the longest, and which is the shortest?

_____

b) How much longer (in cm) is the longest line than the shortest?

_____

67

Find the Perimeter

1)

2)

3)

4)

5)

6)

a) Write down the perimeters for these rectangles (in cm).

_____

b) In millimetres, how big is rectangles 5)'s perimeter?

_____

Gauge the Heat!

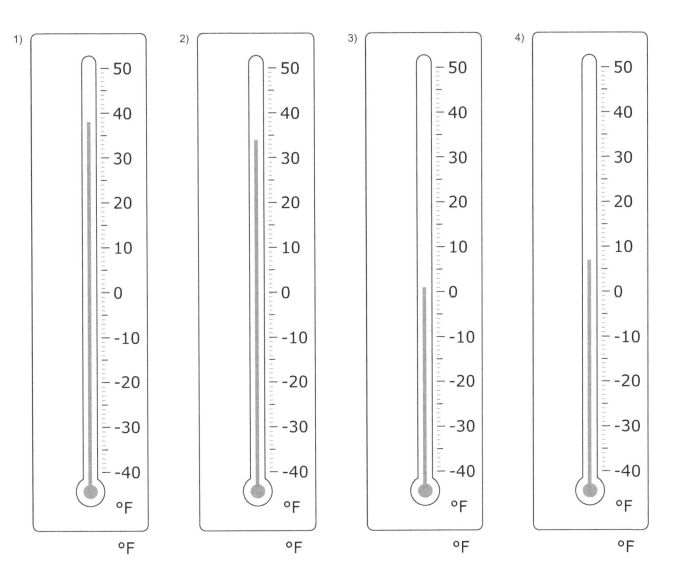

1) °F

2) °F

3) °F

4) °F

a) Write in the temperatures for all the thermometers (in Fahrenheit).

_____

b) Which thermometer is the third hottest?

_____

Gauge the Heat!

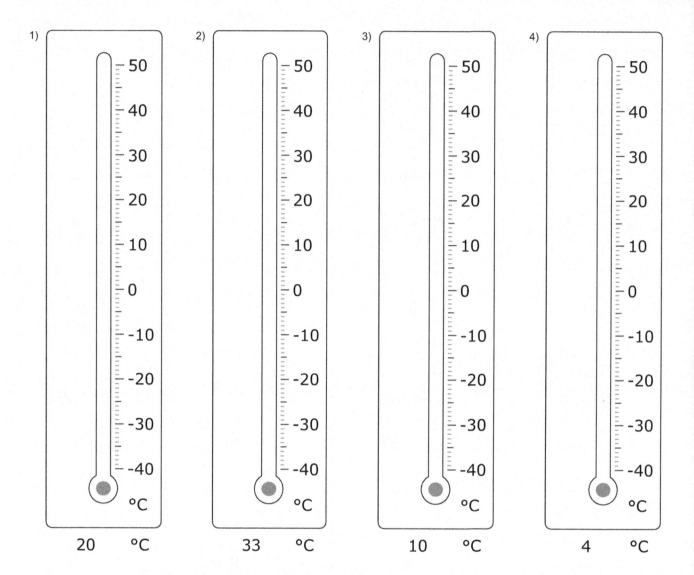

1) 20 °C

2) 33 °C

3) 10 °C

4) 4 °C

a) Shade the thermometers with their correct temperatures (in Celsius).

b) Which thermometer is the hottest and by how much?

_____

c) Which is the coolest thermometer and by how much?

_____

What Time is it?

write the time in the box underneath the clock.

1)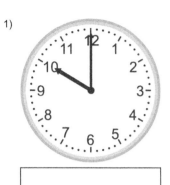

2)

3)

4)

1)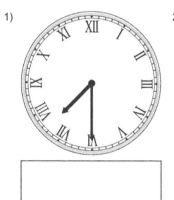

2)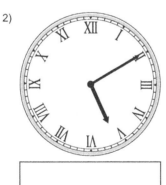

3)

4)

Score: _18_

What Time is it?

write on the clock hands.

1)

| 10:35 | 12:30 | 5:00 | 10:55 |

1) 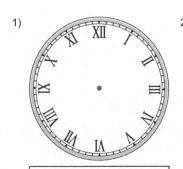 2) 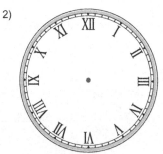 3) 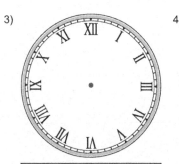 4)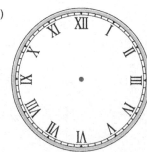

| 10:50 | 7:40 | 10:10 | 3:20 |

Score: _18_

What Time Will It Be?

Draw the clock hands to show the passage of time.

1)

**What time will it be in
4 hours 10 minutes?**

2)

**What time will it be in
2 hours 10 minutes?**

3)

**What time will it be in
2 hours 30 minutes?**

4)

**What time will it be in
5 hours 50 minutes?**

Draw the clock hands to show the passage of time.

1)

What time was it 3 hours 40 minutes ago?

2)

What time was it 3 hours 10 minutes ago?

3)

What time was it 5 hours 0 minutes ago?

4)
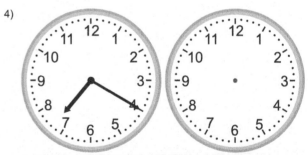

What time was it 5 hours 30 minutes ago?

Charlie is Late!

a) Charlie was meant to arrive home at 3:30pm but arrives at 5:00pm. By how many minutes was he late?

---

b) He then goes to visit a friend at 6 o'clock but he arrives at half past six. By how many minutes was he late?

---

c) Charlie is then meant to be home by 21:00 but arrives at 23:00. By how many hours was he late home?

1) **62 kg =** _____ **g** 2) **98 kg =** _____ **g**

3) **53 kg =** _____ **g** 4) **16 kg =** _____ **g**

5) **10 L =** _____ **mL** 6) **24 L =** _____ **mL**

7) **98 m =** _____ **cm** 8) **87 m =** _____ **cm**

9) **37 cm =** _____ **mm** 10) **41 L =** _____ **mL**

Money as Words

Express the currency values in words.

1) **$860.20** ....

2) **$801.84** ....

3) **$383.64** ....

4) **$427.81** ....

5) **$707.90** ....

6) **$159.41** ....

7) **$414.44** ....

8) **$707.22** ....

9) **$318.35** ....

10) **$387.43** ....

Score: /10

Words as Money

Express these sentences as currency values.

1) .... **one hundred seventy-six dollars sixty-four cents**

2) .... **six hundred sixty dollars twenty cents**

3) .... **two hundred ninety-eight dollars thirty-six cents**

4) .... **seven hundred eighty-nine dollars sixty-four cents**

5) .... **seven hundred sixty-nine dollars seventeen cents**

6) .... **one hundred twenty-nine dollars seventy-four cents**

7) .... **one hundred seventy-five dollars ninety cents**

8) .... **one hundred thirteen dollars thirty-two cents**

9) .... **six hundred seventy-one dollars seventy-one cents**

10) .... **one hundred eighty-six dollars ninety-two cents**

Score: /10

78

Shopping Problems

Solve these shopping problems. The answer bank shows all possible answers.

hot dog = $1.50	cola = $1.00
fries = $1.10	ice cream cone = $1.60
hamburger = $2.20	milk shake = $2.80
deluxe cheeseburger = $3.50	taco = $2.70

1) What is the total cost of a hot dog and a deluxe cheeseburger?

2) If Anish buys an ice cream cone, a fries, and a hamburger, how much money will he get back if he pays $10.00?

3) What is the total cost of a deluxe cheeseburger, a hot dog, and a cola?

4) What is the total cost of a hot dog and a cola?

5) If Max wanted to buy a hot dog, a deluxe cheeseburger, and a taco, how much money would he need?

6) What is the total cost of a cola, a taco, and a hamburger?

7) Adam wants to buy a taco, an ice cream cone, and a deluxe cheeseburger. How much money will he need?

8) What is the total cost of a taco and a milk shake?

9) David wants to buy a milk shake, a cola, and a deluxe cheeseburger. How much money will he need?

0) Charlotte purchases a hamburger, a milk shake, and a deluxe cheeseburger. What will her change be if she pays $20.00?

A. $5.00	B. $7.30	C. $7.80	D. $11.50	E. $2.50	F. $5.10
G. $6.00	H. $7.70	I. $5.90	J. $5.50		

Score: _____ /10

Section 6: Geometry

Name: _____   Date: _____

Class: _____   Teacher: _____

Turns and Angles

Write in the clockwise and anticlockwise turns for each spinner. The first has been done.

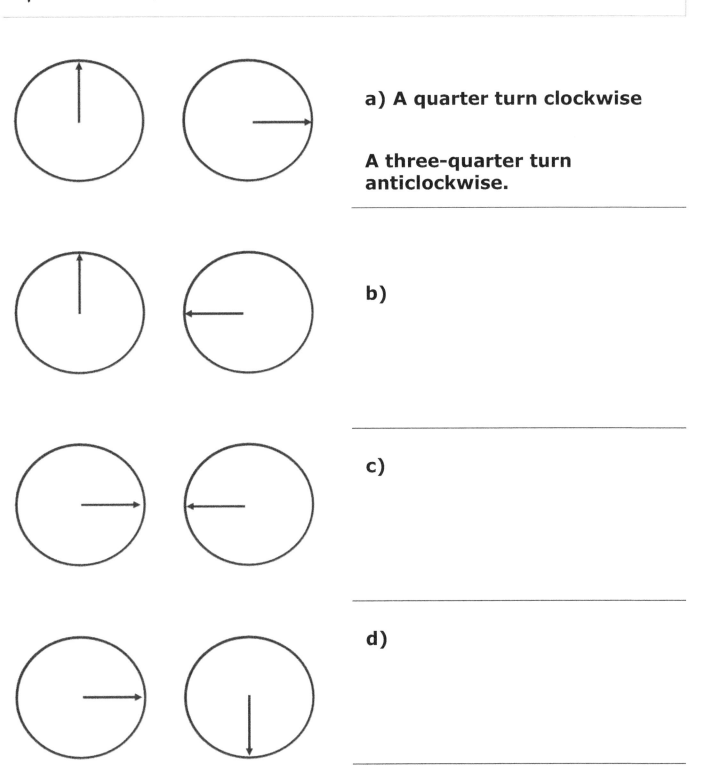

a) A quarter turn clockwise

A three-quarter turn anticlockwise.

b)

c)

d)

Spot the Right Angles

1)

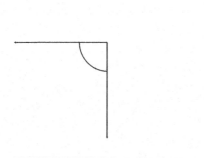

2)

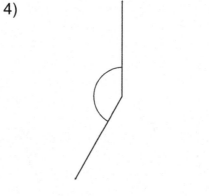

3)

4)

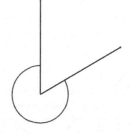

5)

6)

a) Which of the above angles are right angles?

_____

82

Look at an architect's plan for this house.

a) How many right angles can you see on the plan so far?

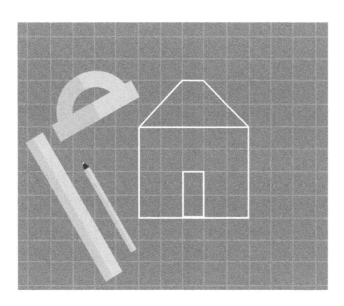

b) The architect has added a chimney to plan. How many right angles are there now?

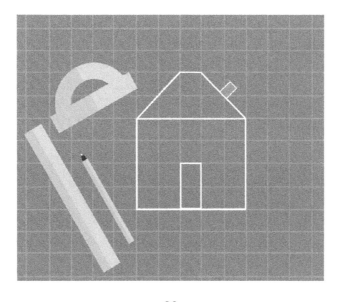

Name the Shape

1)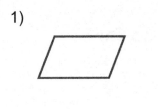

----

2)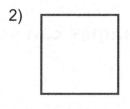

----

3)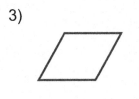

----

4)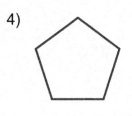

----

5)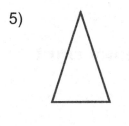

----

6)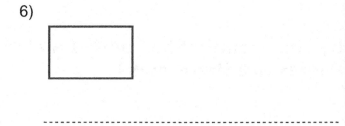

----

7)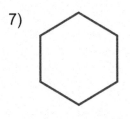

----

8)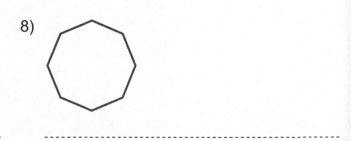

Score: *18*

Name the Shape 2

1)

----

2)

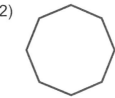

----

3)

----

4)

----

5)

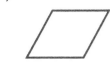

----

6)

----

7)

----

8)

Score: /8

Lines of Symmetry

put the shapes above the table into their correct columns.

Horizontal Lines of Symmetry	Vertical Lines of Symmetry	Horizontal and Vertical Lines of Symmetry

Section 7: Statistics

Name: Date:

Class: Teacher:

Tally Chart 1

Here is a tally chart for a group's favorite animals.

Favorite Animal	Tally	Total
Hippo	卌 IIII	
Toucan	卌 II	
Giraffe	IIII	
Leopard	卌	

a) Write in the totals for all the animals.

b) Which animal is the most popular and which is the least popular?

c) How many more votes would the second most popular animal need to have the most votes?

Tally Chart 2

Finish the tally chart for a classroom's favorite colors.

Favorite Color	Tally	Total
Red		6
Blue		5
Green		10
Yellow		8

a) Write in the tally numbers for all the colors.

b) How many students were in the class?

c) Did more students like either green or blue or did more students either like red or yellow? Show your working.

This bar chart shows the fruit for sale at a supermarket.

1)

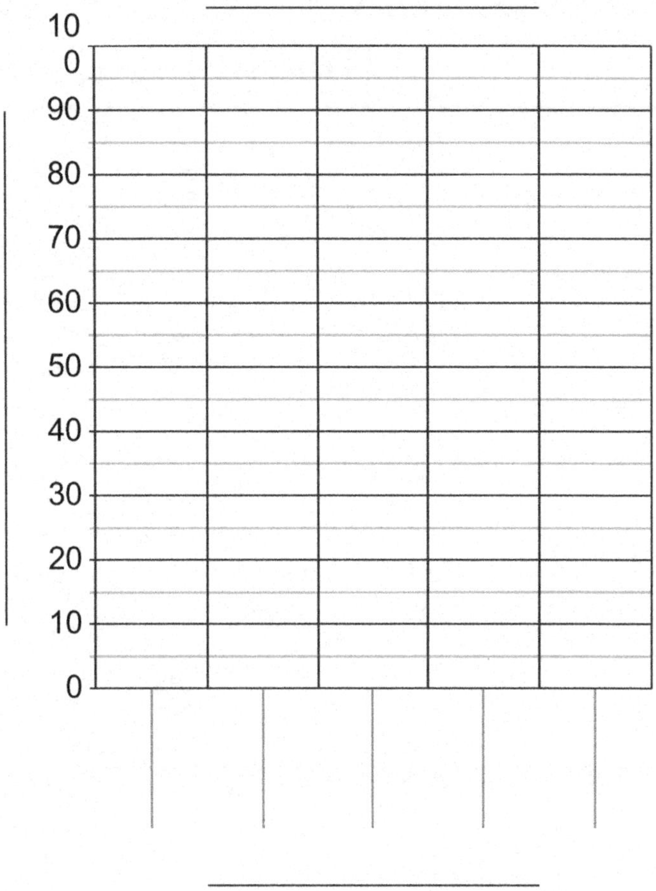

10					
0					
90					
80					
70					
60					
50					
40					
30					
20					
10					
0					

Supermarket Fruit

Fruit	Quantity
Peaches	83
Apples	65
Pears	49
Oranges	36
Plums	57

a) Complete the bar chart adding in the graph title, axis titles and bars.

b) Which fruit does the supermarket have most in stock?

c) Which fruit does the supermarket have the least in stock?

ANSWERS

Section 1
Counting on a Line

30, 70, 10, 75

10   30   70 75

30, 15, 60, 55

15   30   55 60

5, 95, 75, 55

5   55   75   95

20, 60, 35, 55

20   35   55 60

25, 55, 10, 35

10   25   35   55

35, 65, 30, 85

30 35   65   85

27, 147, 127, 67

27   67   127   147

372, 412, 282, 452

282   372   412   452

451, 281, 381, 401

281   381   401   451

882, 902, 812, 792

792 812   882   902

61, 111, 11, 141

11   61   111   141

798, 638, 748, 688

638   688   748   798

Before and After

1) 413 414 415	2) 597 598 599	3) 351 352 353
4) 523 524 525	5) 305 306 307	6) 331 332 333
7) 895 896 897	8) 631 632 633	9) 768 769 770
10) 662 663 664	11) 575 576 577	12) 648 649 650
13) 779 780 781	14) 734 735 736	15) 681 682 683

Circle the Smallest Numbers

1) 775	2) 649	3) (227)	4) 538	5) 975
684	(104)	810	29	778
382	301	528	753	(6)
344	794	657	42	971
(33)	983	516	(23)	575
6) 427	7) 717	8) 849	9) 586	10) 915
(271)	895	799	476	219
886	(4)	930	211	510
983	464	985	(29)	(58)
858	942	(383)	705	709

Circle the Biggest Numbers

1) 193	2) (997)	3) 378	4) 332	5) 739
675	677	218	(806)	99
492	411	318	64	(767)
(892)	769	(936)	714	658
25	605	266	666	437
6) 498	7) 207	8) 41	9) 172	10) 368
566	760	402	(388)	158
(977)	(827)	112	161	275
265	273	438	380	(762)
659	664	(945)	5	373

Circle the Smallest and Biggest Numbers

1) (109)	2) (94)	3) 430	4) (617)	5) (929)
155	(907)	(699)	390	693
795	833	145	(45)	625
392	455	(109)	271	769
(970)	527	398	224	(493)
6) 350	7) 340	8) (51)	9) (133)	10) 472
(937)	291	(965)	569	242
387	(215)	435	657	(51)
653	(891)	302	(911)	(981)
(68)	550	570	514	387

Circle the Odd Numbers

1) (67)	2) (99)	3) (83)	4) (817)	5) (657)
808	432	(63)	668	(507)
818	546	114	962	(679)
(705)	248	(657)	(237)	(789)
(809)	896	(359)	(3)	(527)
6) (849)	7) (907)	8) (31)	9) (117)	10) 722
(121)	776	(451)	662	34
8	(617)	626	702	390
(699)	(543)	(699)	(633)	838
(575)	306	(949)	(33)	256

91

Circle the Even Numbers

1)	2)	3)	4)	5)
97	(738)	(210)	553	313
(268)	(824)	(974)	(866)	(998)
(638)	323	103	(458)	169
319	725	761	209	(206)
283	773	285	(906)	773

6)	7)	8)	9)	10)
35	115	(48)	(116)	73
841	(850)	(550)	785	(460)
(740)	157	209	(148)	(934)
259	435	951	(48)	(964)
(610)	799	(530)	197	641

Numbers as Words

1) 93   ninety-three 2) 60   sixty

3) 51   fifty-one 4) 59   fifty-nine

5) 45   forty-five 6) 94   ninety-four

7) 100   one hundred 8) 34   thirty-four

9) 58   fifty-eight 10) 68   sixty-eight

Words as Numbers

1) 68 sixty-eight 2) 47 forty-seven

3) 19 nineteen 4) 51 fifty-one

5) 99 ninety-nine 6) 88 eighty-eight

7) 73 seventy-three 8) 60 sixty

9) 71 seventy-one 10) 34 thirty-four

Place Values

1) 99$\underline{2}$ = 2 ones 2) 7$\underline{8}$ = 8 ones

3) 80$\underline{7}$ = 7 ones 4) $\underline{9}$11 = 9 hundreds

5) 40$\underline{6}$ = 6 ones 6) 3$\underline{1}$0 = 1 ten

7) 23$\underline{5}$ = 5 ones 8) 1$\underline{1}$3 = 1 ten

9) $\underline{9}$06 = 9 hundreds 10) $\underline{2}$70 = 2 hundreds

Number Comparison

1) 1 < 350 2) 136 < 651 3) 248 < 359

4) 826 > 536 5) 542 > 460 6) 692 > 271

7) 137 < 335 8) 972 > 517 9) 567 > 500

10) 285 < 508 11) 234 < 922 12) 183 > 88

13) 906 > 49 14) 440 < 939 15) 941 > 70

Order the Numbers

1) 177   44 2) 481   68
   246   177   957   210
   892   246   210   481
   504   439   619   553
   439   504   553   619
   44   892   68   957

3) 248   248
   717   420
   674   651
   651   674
   420   676
   676   717

Fill in the Missing Numbers

45	50	55	60	65	70	75	80	85	90

104	112	120	128	136	144	152	160	168	176

50	60	70	80	90	100	110	120	130	140

160	156	152	148	144	140	136	132	128	124

100	150	200	250	300	350	400	450	500	550

100	200	300	400	500	600	700	800	900	1,00

600	550	500	450	400	350	300	250	200	150

84	80	76	72	68	64	60	56	52	48

450	500	550	600	650	700	750	800	850	900

740	730	720	710	700	690	680	670	660	650

Section 2

Pictorial Addition

1) 🍎🍎🍎🍎🍎 + 🍎🍎🍎🍎🍎 = 30
🍎🍎🍎🍎🍎 🍎🍎🍎🍎🍎
🍎🍎🍎 🍎🍎🍎🍎🍎
🍎🍎

2) ★★★★★ + ★★★★★ = 27
★★★★★ ★★★★★
★ ★★★★★
★

3) ♥♥♥♥♥ + ♥♥♥♥♥ = 31
♥♥♥♥♥ ♥♥♥♥♥
♥♥♥♥♥ ♥♥♥♥♥
♥

Part-whole Models

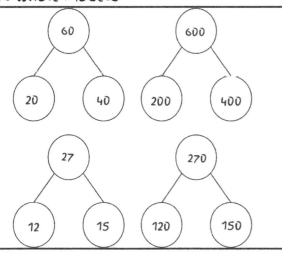

60 → 20, 40

600 → 200, 400

27 → 12, 15

270 → 120, 150

Adding Toucans

10 toucans.

Adding 3 Numbers

1)	8	2)	23	3)	18
	22		11		3
	+ 24		+ 11		+ 9
	54		45		30
4)	8	5)	25	6)	9
	18		26		21
	+ 9		+ 25		+ 22
	35		76		52
7)	24	8)	28	9)	5
	23		16		22
	+ 7		+ 17		+ 9
	54		61		36
10)	4	11)	3	12)	17
	6		19		1
	+ 27		+ 20		+ 24
	37		42		42
13)	23	14)	21	15)	18
	27		18		8
	+ 10		+ 7		+ 25
	60		46		51

Fact Families

1) 85 / 26 59

26 + 59 = 85
59 + 26 = 85
85 - 26 = 59
85 - 59 = 26

2) 73 / 56 17

56 + 17 = 73
17 + 56 = 73
73 - 56 = 17
73 - 17 = 56

3) 74 / 62 12

62 + 12 = 74
12 + 62 = 74
74 - 62 = 12
74 - 12 = 62

4) 94 / 65 29

65 + 29 = 94
29 + 65 = 94
94 - 65 = 29
94 - 29 = 65

Written Questions

a) 770

b) 143

c) 118

d) 221

e) 340

f) 116

Counting Table

1) Count by 5 from 5 to 240

5	10	15	20	25	30
35	40	45	50	55	60
65	70	75	80	85	90
95	100	105	110	115	120
125	130	135	140	145	150
155	160	165	170	175	180
185	190	195	200	205	210
215	220	225	230	235	240

Mixed Operations: Part 1

1) 68 + 14 = 82
2) 25 - 5 = 20
3) 61 + 10 = 71
4) 54 - 10 = 44
5) 35 + 12 = 47
6) 61 + 15 = 76
7) 52 - 9 = 43
8) 99 - 84 = 15
9) 72 - 41 = 31
10) 59 + 24 = 83
11) 47 - 31 = 16
12) 96 - 19 = 77
13) 33 - 8 = 25
14) 15 + 18 = 33
15) 38 - 17 = 21
16) 45 - 25 = 20
17) 13 + 12 = 25
18) 48 + 42 = 90
19) 24 + 28 = 52
20) 14 + 24 = 38

Mixed Operations: Part 2

1)	2)	3)	4)	5)
27 + 46 = 73	61 + 37 = 98	20 - 10 = 10	16 - 11 = 5	13 - 11 = 2
6)	7)	8)	9)	10)
27 + 54 = 81	16 - 12 = 4	55 + 44 = 99	43 + 46 = 89	13 - 13 = 0
11)	12)	13)	14)	15)
17 - 16 = 1	25 + 68 = 93	11 - 10 = 1	18 - 17 = 1	26 + 57 = 83
16)	17)	18)	19)	20)
52 + 35 = 87	12 - 10 = 2	49 + 22 = 71	19 - 11 = 8	15 - 10 = 5
21)	22)	23)	24)	25)
17 - 10 = 7	31 + 66 = 97	33 + 66 = 99	17 - 15 = 2	17 - 14 = 3
26)	27)	28)	29)	30)
18 - 14 = 4	49 + 31 = 80	55 + 43 = 98	40 + 54 = 94	51 + 30 = 81

Charlie Croc!

Left side: 160
Right side: 350

95 + 130 = 225

Adding Numbers 0-1000: Part 1

1)	2)	3)	4)	5)
260 + 10 = 270	482 + 10 = 492	414 + 30 = 444	122 + 50 = 172	224 + 10 = 234
6)	7)	8)	9)	10)
297 + 20 = 317	481 + 50 = 531	264 + 40 = 304	391 + 10 = 401	222 + 50 = 272
11)	12)	13)	14)	15)
384 + 60 = 444	461 + 30 = 491	216 + 60 = 276	500 + 10 = 510	490 + 10 = 500
16)	17)	18)	19)	20)
207 + 50 = 257	168 + 70 = 238	198 + 20 = 218	407 + 70 = 477	298 + 40 = 338

Adding Numbers 0-1000: Part 2

1)	2)	3)	4)	5)
192 + 100 = 292	464 + 400 = 864	450 + 300 = 750	204 + 500 = 704	417 + 100 = 517
6)	7)	8)	9)	10)
204 + 500 = 704	387 + 400 = 787	284 + 400 = 684	257 + 100 = 357	128 + 200 = 328
11)	12)	13)	14)	15)
160 + 200 = 360	307 + 300 = 607	303 + 100 = 403	446 + 400 = 846	329 + 400 = 729
16)	17)	18)	19)	20)
188 + 400 = 588	282 + 200 = 482	400 + 400 = 800	384 + 500 = 884	256 + 500 = 756

Subtracting Numbers 0-1000: Part 1

1)	2)	3)	4)	5)
252 - 40 = 212	619 - 60 = 559	238 - 30 = 208	288 - 30 = 258	126 - 60 = 66
6)	7)	8)	9)	10)
571 - 30 = 541	306 - 70 = 236	308 - 40 = 268	306 - 70 = 236	432 - 60 = 372
11)	12)	13)	14)	15)
640 - 10 = 630	812 - 60 = 752	560 - 10 = 550	428 - 70 = 358	207 - 70 = 137
16)	17)	18)	19)	20)
457 - 70 = 387	347 - 10 = 337	477 - 70 = 407	603 - 40 = 563	456 - 50 = 406

Subtracting Numbers 0-1000: Part 2

1)	2)	3)	4)	5)
595 - 100 = 495	287 - 100 = 187	817 - 700 = 117	531 - 300 = 231	873 - 200 = 673
6)	7)	8)	9)	10)
780 - 500 = 280	849 - 700 = 149	331 - 100 = 231	851 - 300 = 551	680 - 500 = 180
11)	12)	13)	14)	15)
599 - 400 = 199	649 - 400 = 249	872 - 700 = 172	341 - 100 = 241	836 - 100 = 736
16)	17)	18)	19)	20)
771 - 500 = 271	691 - 400 = 291	668 - 200 = 468	493 - 100 = 393	599 - 400 = 199

Mixed Operations 0-1000

1)	2)	3)	4)	5)
382 + 190 = 572	613 - 257 = 356	499 + 259 = 758	465 - 254 = 211	238 + 127 = 365
6)	7)	8)	9)	10)
252 + 701 = 953	579 + 401 = 980	650 - 311 = 339	760 - 272 = 488	208 + 331 = 539
11)	12)	13)	14)	15)
448 - 297 = 151	328 - 177 = 151	646 + 208 = 854	965 - 141 = 824	746 - 469 = 277
16)	17)	18)	19)	20)
301 + 409 = 710	550 - 178 = 372	646 - 185 = 461	206 + 198 = 404	154 + 165 = 319
21)	22)	23)	24)	25)
883 - 184 = 699	671 + 229 = 900	615 - 173 = 442	499 - 301 = 198	653 + 152 = 805
26)	27)	28)	29)	30)
111 + 775 = 886	755 - 394 = 361	412 + 540 = 952	502 - 107 = 395	155 + 725 = 880

Section 3

Multiplying by 1-4: Part 1

1) 1 × 12 = 12	2) 3 × 12 = 36	3) 2 × 5 = 10	4) 2 × 10 = 20	5) 3 × 4 = 12
6) 3 × 11 = 33	7) 3 × 2 = 6	8) 1 × 11 = 11	9) 3 × 9 = 27	10) 4 × 11 = 44
11) 1 × 10 = 10	12) 4 × 7 = 28	13) 2 × 4 = 8	14) 4 × 10 = 40	15) 2 × 3 = 6
16) 4 × 4 = 16	17) 2 × 11 = 22	18) 3 × 8 = 24	19) 2 × 8 = 16	20) 3 × 10 = 30
21) 1 × 4 = 4	22) 4 × 8 = 32	23) 3 × 5 = 15	24) 3 × 3 = 9	25) 4 × 9 = 36
26) 3 × 1 = 3	27) 2 × 12 = 24	28) 3 × 6 = 18	29) 3 × 7 = 21	30) 4 × 3 = 12
31) 2 × 2 = 4	32) 1 × 6 = 6	33) 1 × 8 = 8	34) 4 × 6 = 24	35) 2 × 9 = 18
36) 4 × 2 = 8	37) 4 × 5 = 20	38) 1 × 7 = 7	39) 2 × 7 = 14	40) 1 × 1 = 1

Multiplying by 1-4: Part 2

1) 5 × 3 = 15	2) 4 × 2 = 8	3) 8 × 2 = 16	4) 11 × 4 = 44	5) 2 × 4 = 8
6) 9 × 2 = 18	7) 6 × 2 = 12	8) 7 × 1 = 7	9) 10 × 4 = 40	10) 2 × 2 = 4
11) 1 × 3 = 3	12) 4 × 3 = 12	13) 12 × 2 = 24	14) 7 × 4 = 28	15) 3 × 3 = 9
16) 10 × 1 = 10	17) 8 × 4 = 32	18) 5 × 1 = 5	19) 7 × 2 = 14	20) 10 × 2 = 20
21) 8 × 3 = 24	22) 1 × 4 = 4	23) 8 × 1 = 8	24) 5 × 2 = 10	25) 12 × 4 = 48
26) 3 × 2 = 6	27) 9 × 4 = 36	28) 2 × 3 = 6	29) 9 × 3 = 27	30) 7 × 3 = 21
31) 11 × 3 = 33	32) 2 × 1 = 2	33) 9 × 1 = 9	34) 10 × 3 = 30	35) 11 × 2 = 22
36) 3 × 4 = 12	37) 6 × 4 = 24	38) 6 × 3 = 18	39) 12 × 3 = 36	40) 5 × 4 = 20

The Tree

Possible Sums: 3 x 4 = 12, 4 x 3 = 12, 6 x 2 = 12 and 2 x 6 = 12

Multiplying by 5-8: Part 1

1) 7 × 10 = 70	2) 7 × 5 = 35	3) 7 × 11 = 77	4) 6 × 4 = 24	5) 6 × 3 = 18
6) 7 × 2 = 14	7) 5 × 5 = 25	8) 6 × 11 = 66	9) 6 × 8 = 48	10) 8 × 3 = 24
11) 6 × 10 = 60	12) 6 × 5 = 30	13) 5 × 4 = 20	14) 6 × 7 = 42	15) 8 × 11 = 88
16) 8 × 8 = 64	17) 8 × 10 = 80	18) 6 × 12 = 72	19) 8 × 9 = 72	20) 8 × 4 = 32
21) 8 × 12 = 96	22) 7 × 7 = 49	23) 7 × 4 = 28	24) 6 × 9 = 54	25) 7 × 12 = 84
26) 7 × 1 = 7	27) 5 × 10 = 50	28) 7 × 6 = 42	29) 6 × 6 = 36	30) 5 × 11 = 55
31) 7 × 8 = 56	32) 5 × 12 = 60	33) 6 × 2 = 12	34) 8 × 6 = 48	35) 6 × 1 = 6
36) 8 × 5 = 40	37) 5 × 7 = 35	38) 8 × 7 = 56	39) 5 × 1 = 5	40) 8 × 1 = 8

Multiplying by 5-8: Part 1

1) 2 × 6 = 12	2) 3 × 6 = 18	3) 6 × 7 = 42	4) 4 × 5 = 20	5) 1 × 5 = 5
6) 9 × 8 = 72	7) 7 × 5 = 35	8) 3 × 7 = 21	9) 2 × 8 = 16	10) 4 × 8 = 32
11) 11 × 6 = 66	12) 1 × 6 = 6	13) 7 × 7 = 49	14) 11 × 8 = 88	15) 11 × 7 = 77
16) 6 × 5 = 30	17) 10 × 6 = 60	18) 12 × 7 = 84	19) 5 × 6 = 30	20) 9 × 7 = 63
21) 2 × 5 = 10	22) 9 × 6 = 54	23) 8 × 8 = 64	24) 3 × 8 = 24	25) 6 × 6 = 36
26) 1 × 8 = 8	27) 3 × 5 = 15	28) 7 × 6 = 42	29) 12 × 6 = 72	30) 10 × 7 = 70
31) 8 × 7 = 56	32) 5 × 8 = 40	33) 4 × 7 = 28	34) 8 × 6 = 48	35) 7 × 8 = 56
36) 9 × 5 = 45	37) 4 × 6 = 24	38) 2 × 7 = 14	39) 11 × 5 = 55	40) 8 × 5 = 40

Multiplication: Bullseye

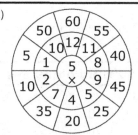

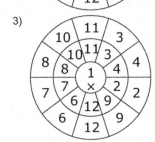

Multiplying by 9-12: Part 1

1) 11 ×12 = 132	2) 11 × 8 = 88	3) 10 × 2 = 20	4) 10 × 7 = 70	5) 11 × 7 = 77
6) 10 × 11 = 110	7) 12 × 5 = 60	8) 9 × 7 = 63	9) 9 × 6 = 54	10) 11 × 4 = 44
11) 10 × 10 = 100	12) 10 × 12 = 120	13) 11 × 2 = 22	14) 9 × 3 = 27	15) 10 × 6 = 60
16) 11 × 11 = 121	17) 12 × 6 = 72	18) 11 × 5 = 55	19) 10 × 9 = 90	20) 10 × 5 = 50
21) 12 × 4 = 48	22) 11 × 1 = 11	23) 12 × 8 = 96	24) 9 × 11 = 99	25) 9 × 10 = 90
26) 12 × 12 = 144	27) 9 × 12 = 108	28) 12 × 11 = 132	29) 11 × 6 = 66	30) 11 × 10 = 110
31) 12 × 10 = 120	32) 12 × 3 = 36	33) 11 × 9 = 99	34) 10 × 1 = 10	35) 12 × 1 = 12
36) 11 × 3 = 33	37) 9 × 2 = 18	38) 10 × 4 = 40	39) 9 × 5 = 45	40) 12 × 7 = 84

Multiplying by 9-12: Part 2

1) 7 × 10 = 70	2) 9 × 10 = 90	3) 3 × 12 = 36	4) 5 × 12 = 60	5) 4 × 11 = 44
6) 11 × 10 = 110	7) 3 × 10 = 30	8) 5 × 10 = 50	9) 2 × 12 = 24	10) 7 × 11 = 77
11) 8 × 10 = 80	12) 10 × 11 = 110	13) 6 × 11 = 66	14) 8 × 12 = 96	15) 6 × 9 = 54
16) 2 × 11 = 22	17) 3 × 11 = 33	18) 10 × 12 = 120	19) 1 × 10 = 10	20) 9 × 9 = 81
21) 12 × 11 = 132	22) 1 × 11 = 11	23) 2 × 10 = 20	24) 8 × 11 = 88	25) 4 × 9 = 36
26) 12 × 10 = 120	27) 6 × 12 = 72	28) 6 × 10 = 60	29) 7 × 9 = 63	30) 4 × 12 = 48
31) 11 × 11 = 121	32) 11 × 12 = 132	33) 4 × 10 = 40	34) 10 × 10 = 100	35) 10 × 9 = 90
36) 7 × 12 = 84	37) 9 × 11 = 99	38) 11 × 9 = 99	39) 9 × 12 = 108	40) 5 × 11 = 55

Multiplication Word Problems

1) 24 2) 20 3) 16 4) 12 5) 40

Dividing by 1-5

1) 9 ÷ 1 = 9	2) 10 ÷ 5 = 2
3) 6 ÷ 3 = 2	4) 12 ÷ 4 = 3
5) 27 ÷ 3 = 9	6) 3 ÷ 1 = 3
7) 9 ÷ 3 = 3	8) 6 ÷ 1 = 6
9) 8 ÷ 4 = 2	10) 35 ÷ 5 = 7
11) 15 ÷ 3 = 5	12) 32 ÷ 4 = 8
13) 36 ÷ 4 = 9	14) 28 ÷ 4 = 7
15) 8 ÷ 1 = 8	16) 18 ÷ 2 = 9
17) 24 ÷ 4 = 6	18) 8 ÷ 2 = 4
19) 30 ÷ 3 = 10	20) 5 ÷ 1 = 5

Dividing by 6-10

1) $64 \div 8 = 8$
2) $56 \div 8 = 7$
3) $9 \div 9 = 1$
4) $14 \div 7 = 2$
5) $36 \div 9 = 4$
6) $72 \div 8 = 9$
7) $40 \div 8 = 5$
8) $80 \div 10 = 8$
9) $81 \div 9 = 9$
10) $16 \div 8 = 2$
11) $32 \div 8 = 4$
12) $35 \div 7 = 5$
13) $60 \div 6 = 10$
14) $48 \div 6 = 8$
15) $12 \div 6 = 2$
16) $49 \div 7 = 7$
17) $90 \div 9 = 10$
18) $60 \div 10 = 6$
19) $72 \div 9 = 8$
20) $63 \div 9 = 7$

Division Word Problems

1) 8 2) 9 3) 9 4) 6 5) 5

Fact Families

1)

$4 \times 3 = 12$
$3 \times 4 = 12$
$12 \div 4 = 3$
$12 \div 3 = 4$

2)

$2 \times 3 = 6$
$3 \times 2 = 6$
$6 \div 2 = 3$
$6 \div 3 = 2$

3)

$7 \times 5 = 35$
$5 \times 7 = 35$
$35 \div 7 = 5$
$35 \div 5 = 7$

4)

$4 \times 2 = 8$
$2 \times 4 = 8$
$8 \div 4 = 2$
$8 \div 2 = 4$

The Maze!

From the left:

$7 \times 5 = 35$
$10 \times 3 = 30$
$26 \div 2 = 13$
$5 \times 9 = 45$
$63 \div 7 = 9$
$5 \times 6 = 30$
$8 \times 9 = 72$
$11 \times 5 = 55$

Right or Wrong?

The following sums are incorrect:
$32 \div 4 = 7$
$10 \times 2 = 18$
$16 \div 5 = 4$
$3 \times 4 = 9$

Section 4

Shading Shapes

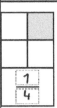

a) The fourth set of blocks (on the far right) represents one whole.

b) Shade in any combination of two individual squares.

Shade the Fraction

1) $\frac{1}{3}$ =
2) $\frac{1}{8}$ =
3) $\frac{1}{2}$ =
4) $\frac{2}{3}$ =
5) $\frac{1}{5}$ =
6) $\frac{1}{4}$ =
7) $\frac{4}{6}$ =
8) $\frac{3}{8}$ =
9) $\frac{4}{5}$ =
10) $\frac{7}{8}$ =

Identify the Shaded Fraction

1) $= \frac{1}{5}$
2) $= \frac{2}{4}$
3) $= \frac{1}{3}$
4) $= \frac{3}{8}$
5) $= \frac{3}{6}$
6) $= \frac{3}{5}$
7) $= \frac{3}{4}$
8) $= \frac{5}{8}$
9) $= \frac{2}{6}$
10) $= \frac{1}{2}$

Charlie's Pizza

a) Initially Charlie eats 1/2 (a half of the pizza.
b) He then eats a half of the remaining pizza. So he is now left with a quarter (1/4) of his pizza.

Charlie's Journey

a) Initially Charlie travels 4 out of 16 miles, so he has travelled a quarter (1/4) of his journey.
b) He then travels 10 miles further. He has now completed 14 out of 16 miles, 7/8 of his journey.

Fractions on a Line

1)
$$1\frac{1}{2} \quad \frac{1}{2} \quad \frac{3}{4} \quad 1\frac{1}{4}$$

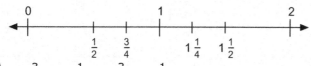

2)
$$1\frac{3}{4} \quad \frac{1}{4} \quad \frac{3}{4} \quad \frac{1}{2}$$

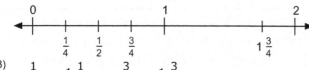

3)
$$\frac{1}{4} \quad 1\frac{1}{4} \quad \frac{3}{4} \quad 1\frac{3}{4}$$

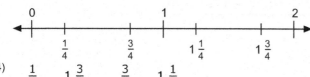

4)
$$\frac{1}{4} \quad 1\frac{3}{4} \quad \frac{3}{4} \quad 1\frac{1}{4}$$

0 ◄——┼——┼——┼——┼——┼——► 2
$\frac{1}{4}$ $\frac{3}{4}$ $1\frac{1}{4}$ $1\frac{3}{4}$

Add the Fractions

1) $\frac{1}{10} + \frac{7}{10} = \frac{8}{10}$ 2) $\frac{2}{10} + \frac{1}{10} = \frac{3}{10}$

3) $\frac{9}{10} + \frac{3}{10} = \frac{12}{10}$ 4) $\frac{8}{10} + \frac{3}{10} = \frac{11}{10}$

5) $\frac{6}{10} + \frac{3}{10} = \frac{9}{10}$ 6) $\frac{5}{10} + \frac{7}{10} = \frac{12}{10}$

7) $\frac{8}{10} + \frac{1}{10} = \frac{9}{10}$ 8) $\frac{1}{10} + \frac{1}{10} = \frac{2}{10}$

9) $\frac{5}{10} + \frac{1}{10} = \frac{6}{10}$ 10) $\frac{9}{10} + \frac{9}{10} = \frac{18}{10}$

Add the Fractions 2

1) $\frac{2}{4} + \frac{3}{4} = \frac{5}{4}$ 2) $\frac{1}{3} + \frac{2}{3} = \frac{1}{1}$ 3) $\frac{4}{5} + \frac{4}{5} = \frac{8}{5}$ 4) $\frac{4}{6} + \frac{1}{6} = \frac{5}{6}$ 5) $\frac{1}{2} + \frac{1}{2} = \frac{1}{1}$

6) $\frac{2}{4} + \frac{1}{4} = \frac{3}{4}$ 7) $\frac{2}{5} + \frac{4}{5} = \frac{6}{5}$ 8) $\frac{2}{3} + \frac{2}{3} = \frac{4}{3}$ 9) $\frac{1}{4} + \frac{1}{4} = \frac{1}{2}$ 10) $\frac{1}{3} + \frac{1}{3} = \frac{1}{1}$

11) $\frac{2}{5} + \frac{3}{5} = \frac{1}{1}$ 12) $\frac{1}{6} + \frac{1}{6} = \frac{1}{3}$ 13) $\frac{3}{4} + \frac{1}{4} = \frac{1}{1}$ 14) $\frac{3}{6} + \frac{1}{6} = \frac{2}{3}$ 15) $\frac{3}{5} + \frac{4}{5} = \frac{7}{5}$

16) $\frac{3}{6} + \frac{5}{6} = \frac{4}{3}$ 17) $\frac{2}{5} + \frac{1}{5} = \frac{3}{5}$ 18) $\frac{4}{5} + \frac{3}{5} = \frac{7}{5}$ 19) $\frac{5}{6} + \frac{1}{6} = \frac{1}{1}$ 20) $\frac{1}{5} + \frac{4}{5} = \frac{1}{1}$

Group the Rhinos

a) There are 2 sets of 6 rhinos.
b) You could split each group of 6 into:
i) 2 sets of 3
ii) 3 sets of 2

Simplifying Fractions

1) $\frac{14}{28} = \frac{1}{2}$ 2) $\frac{12}{16} = \frac{3}{4}$ 3) $\frac{3}{9} = \frac{1}{3}$ 4) $\frac{2}{12} = \frac{1}{6}$

5) $\frac{24}{48} = \frac{1}{2}$ 6) $\frac{10}{25} = \frac{2}{5}$ 7) $\frac{6}{8} = \frac{3}{4}$ 8) $\frac{2}{6} = \frac{1}{3}$

9) $\frac{9}{15} = \frac{3}{5}$ 10) $\frac{27}{54} = \frac{1}{2}$ 11) $\frac{35}{40} = \frac{7}{8}$ 12) $\frac{40}{48} = \frac{5}{6}$

13) $\frac{6}{12} = \frac{1}{2}$ 14) $\frac{18}{30} = \frac{3}{5}$ 15) $\frac{9}{24} = \frac{3}{8}$ 16) $\frac{12}{18} = \frac{2}{3}$

17) $\frac{16}{48} = \frac{1}{3}$ 18) $\frac{5}{15} = \frac{1}{3}$ 19) $\frac{12}{48} = \frac{1}{4}$ 20) $\frac{4}{10} = \frac{2}{5}$

Equivalent Fractions

1) $\frac{2}{3} = \frac{16}{24}$ 2) $\frac{1}{4} = \frac{8}{32}$ 3) $\frac{1}{4} = \frac{10}{40}$ 4) $\frac{1}{3} = \frac{8}{24}$

5) $\frac{1}{4} = \frac{6}{24}$ 6) $\frac{2}{4} = \frac{10}{20}$ 7) $\frac{1}{3} = \frac{10}{30}$ 8) $\frac{1}{4} = \frac{9}{36}$

9) $\frac{1}{3} = \frac{5}{15}$ 10) $\frac{2}{4} = \frac{6}{12}$ 11) $\frac{2}{3} = \frac{18}{27}$ 12) $\frac{3}{4} = \frac{24}{32}$

13) $\frac{1}{3} = \frac{7}{21}$ 14) $\frac{1}{3} = \frac{2}{6}$ 15) $\frac{2}{3} = \frac{14}{21}$ 16) $\frac{2}{4} = \frac{12}{24}$

17) $\frac{2}{3} = \frac{12}{18}$ 18) $\frac{2}{4} = \frac{16}{32}$ 19) $\frac{1}{3} = \frac{3}{9}$ 20) $\frac{3}{4} = \frac{21}{28}$

Comparing Fractions

1) $\frac{3}{6} = \frac{2}{4}$ 2) $\frac{7}{8} > \frac{1}{8}$ 3) $\frac{3}{6} > \frac{1}{4}$ 4) $\frac{1}{3} < \frac{2}{5}$

5) $\frac{1}{3} < \frac{4}{6}$ 6) $\frac{2}{5} < \frac{3}{4}$ 7) $\frac{7}{8} > \frac{3}{4}$ 8) $\frac{4}{6} < \frac{7}{8}$

9) $\frac{3}{5} > \frac{1}{4}$ 10) $\frac{4}{6} > \frac{1}{3}$ 11) $\frac{5}{8} < \frac{4}{5}$ 12) $\frac{1}{8} < \frac{1}{3}$

13) $\frac{3}{5} < \frac{3}{4}$ 14) $\frac{5}{6} > \frac{2}{4}$ 15) $\frac{5}{8} < \frac{2}{3}$ 16) $\frac{2}{5} < \frac{5}{6}$

17) $\frac{4}{5} > \frac{2}{3}$ 18) $\frac{3}{4} < \frac{7}{8}$ 19) $\frac{4}{6} > \frac{2}{4}$ 20) $\frac{3}{6} < \frac{2}{3}$

Translating Fractions to Whole Numbers

1) $\frac{1}{3}$ of 6 = 2   2) $\frac{1}{5}$ of 5 = 1

3) $\frac{1}{6}$ of 6 = 1   4) $\frac{1}{4}$ of 8 = 2

5) $\frac{6}{8}$ of 8 = 6   6) $\frac{6}{10}$ of 10 = 6

7) $\frac{1}{2}$ of 4 = 2   8) $\frac{2}{3}$ of 3 = 2

9) $\frac{13}{20}$ of 20 = 13   10) $\frac{4}{6}$ of 6 = 4

11) $\frac{1}{2}$ of 6 = 3   12) $\frac{2}{5}$ of 5 = 2

13) $\frac{1}{4}$ of 4 = 1   14) $\frac{4}{8}$ of 8 = 4

15) $\frac{2}{10}$ of 10 = 2   16) $\frac{2}{3}$ of 6 = 4

17) $\frac{3}{20}$ of 20 = 3   18) $\frac{8}{10}$ of 10 = 8

19) $\frac{3}{6}$ of 6 = 3   20) $\frac{6}{20}$ of 20 = 6

Shade the Fractions

1) 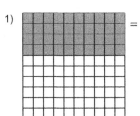 $= \frac{2}{5}$ 2) 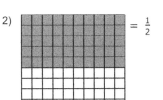 $= \frac{1}{2}$

3) 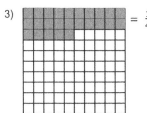 $= \frac{1}{4}$ 4) 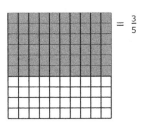 $= \frac{3}{5}$

5) 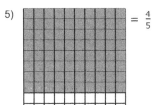 $= \frac{4}{5}$ 6) 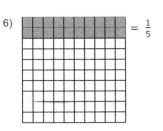 $= \frac{1}{5}$

Identify the Fractions

1) 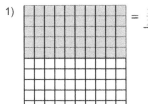 $= \frac{1}{2}$ 2) 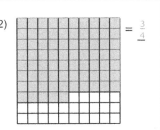 $= \frac{3}{4}$

3) 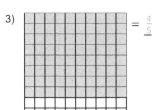 $= \frac{4}{5}$ 4) 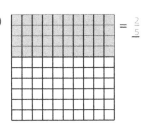 $= \frac{2}{5}$

5) 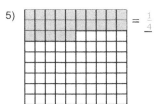 $= \frac{1}{4}$ 6) 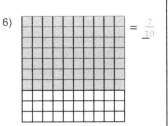 $= \frac{7}{10}$

Section 5

Measuring Lines

a) Line 5 (17cm) is the longest and Line 7 (3cm) is the shortest.
b) 14cm longer.

Find the Perimeter

a) 1) 18cm; 2) 14cm; 3) 12cm; 4) 16cm; 5) 18cm; 6) 16cm
b) 180mm

Gauge the Heat

1) 38°F 2) 34°F 3) 1°F 4) 7°F
4) is third hottest.

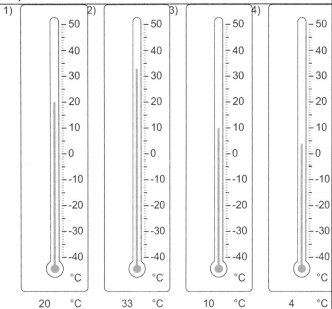

b) 2 is the hottest by 13°c

c) 4 is the coolest by 6°c

What Time is it? (Write the time)

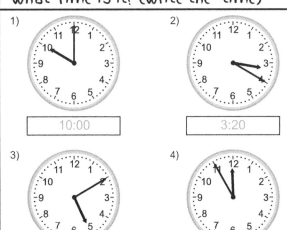

1) 10:00 2) 3:20

3) 5:10 4) 11:55

99

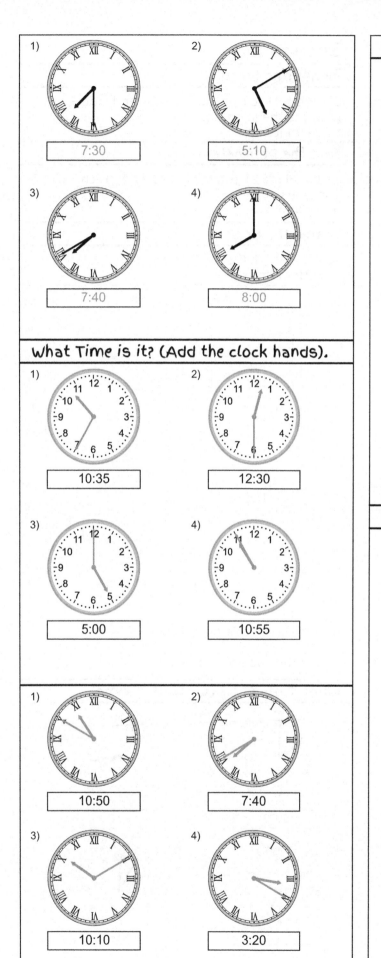

What Time is it? (Add the clock hands).

1) 10:35
2) 12:30
3) 5:00
4) 10:55

1) 10:50
2) 7:40
3) 10:10
4) 3:20

1)  **What time will it be in 4 hours 10 minutes?**

2)  **What time will it be in 2 hours 10 minutes?**

3) **What time will it be in 2 hours 30 minutes?**

4) **What time will it be in 5 hours 50 minutes?**

What Time was it?

1)  **What time was it 3 hours 40 minutes ago?**

2)  **What time was it 3 hours 10 minutes ago?**

3) **What time was it 5 hours 0 minutes ago?**

4)  **What time was it 5 hours 30 minutes ago?**

Charlie is Late!

a) 90 minutes late.
b) 30 minutes late.
c) 2 hours late.

Conversions

1) 62 kg = 62,000 g   2) 98 kg = 98,000 g

3) 53 kg = 53,000 g   4) 16 kg = 16,000 g

5) 10 L = 10,000 mL   6) 24 L = 24,000 mL

7) 98 m = 9,800 cm   8) 87 m = 8,700 cm

9) 37 cm = 370 mm   10) 41 L = 41,000 mL

Money as Words

1) $860.20=eight hundred sixty dollars twenty cents

2) $801.84=eight hundred one dollars eighty-four cents

3) $383.64=three hundred eighty-three dollars sixty-four cents

4) $427.81=four hundred twenty-seven dollars eighty-one cents

5) $707.90=seven hundred seven dollars ninety cents

6) $159.41=one hundred fifty-nine dollars forty-one cents

7) $414.44=four hundred fourteen dollars forty-four cents

8) $707.22=seven hundred seven dollars twenty-two cents

9) $318.35=three hundred eighteen dollars thirty-five cents

10) $387.43=three hundred eighty-seven dollars forty-three cents

Words as Money

1) $176.64=one hundred seventy-six dollars sixty-four cents

2) $660.20=six hundred sixty dollars twenty cents

3) $298.36=two hundred ninety-eight dollars thirty-six cents

4) $789.64=seven hundred eighty-nine dollars sixty-four cents

5) $769.17=seven hundred sixty-nine dollars seventeen cents

6) $129.74=one hundred twenty-nine dollars seventy-four cents

7) $175.90=one hundred seventy-five dollars ninety cents

8) $113.32=one hundred thirteen dollars thirty-two cents

9) $671.71=six hundred seventy-one dollars seventy-one cents

10) $186.92=one hundred eighty-six dollars ninety-two cents

Shopping Problems

1) $5.00 2) $5.10 3) $6.00 4) $2.50 5) $7.70
6) $5.90 7) $7.80 8) $5.50 9) $7.30
10) $11.50

Section 6

Turns and Angles

a) A quarter turn clockwise
A three-quarter turn anticlockwise.

b) A three-quarter turn clockwise
A quarter turn anticlockwise.

c) A half-turn clockwise
A half-turn anticlockwise.

d) A quarter turn clockwise
A three-quarter turn anticlockwise.

Spot the Right Angles

Angles 3) and 5) are right angles.

Building a House

a) 10 right angles

b) 14 right angles with the chimney.

Name the Shape

1)
Parallelogram

2)
Square

3)
Rhombus

4)
Regular Pentagon

5)
Isosceles Triangle

6)
Rectangle

7)
Regular Hexagon

8)
Regular Octagon

Name the Shape 2

1)
Rectangle

2)
Regular Octagon

3)
Equilateral Triangle

4)
Isosceles Triangle

5)
Rhombus

6)
Parallelogram

7)
Regular Hexagon

8)
Trapezoid

Lines of Symmetry

Horizontal Lines of Symmetry	Vertical Lines of Symmetry	Horizontal and Vertical Lines of Symmetry

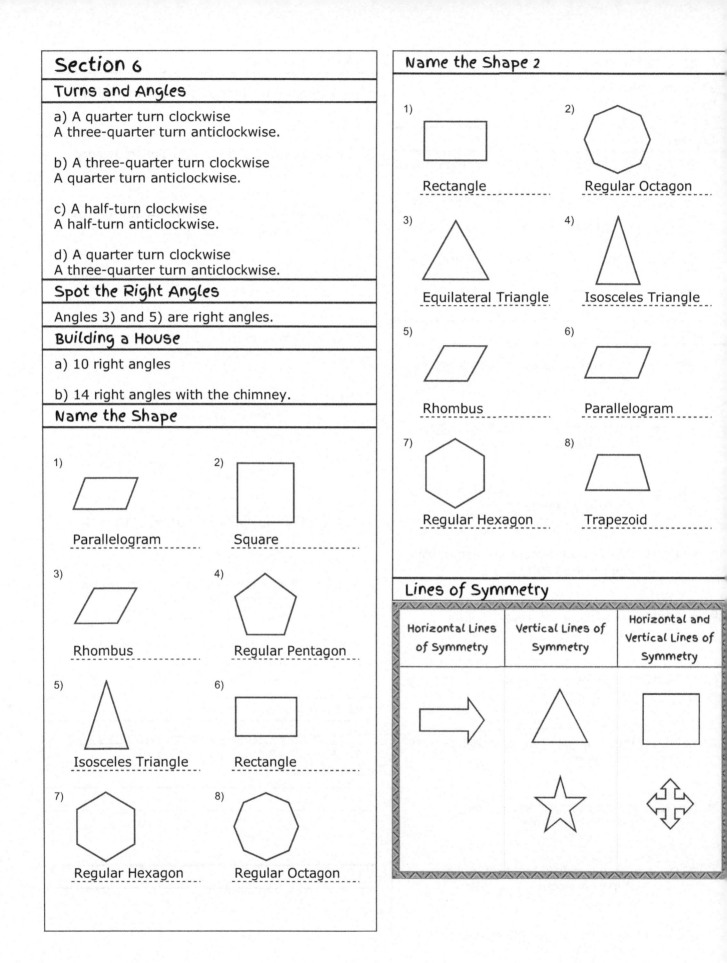

Section 7

Tally Chart 1

Favorite Animal	Tally	Total
Hippo	𝍸𝍸𝍸𝍸𝍸 ||||	9
Toucan	𝍸𝍸𝍸𝍸𝍸 ||	7
Giraffe	||||	4
Leopard	𝍸𝍸𝍸𝍸𝍸	5

b) Hippos (9 votes) are the most popular and Giraffes (4) are the least popular.

b) The toucan (7 votes) would need 3 more votes to overtake the hippo (9).

Tally Chart 2

Favorite Color	Tally	Total
Red	𝍸𝍸𝍸𝍸𝍸		6
Blue	𝍸𝍸𝍸𝍸𝍸	5
Green	𝍸𝍸𝍸𝍸𝍸 𝍸𝍸𝍸𝍸𝍸	10
Yellow	𝍸𝍸𝍸𝍸𝍸 |||	8

b) There are 29 students in the class.

c) 15 (10 + 5) students liked green or blue

14 students (6 + 8) liked red or yellow.

Therefore, more students liked either green or blue.

Bar Chart

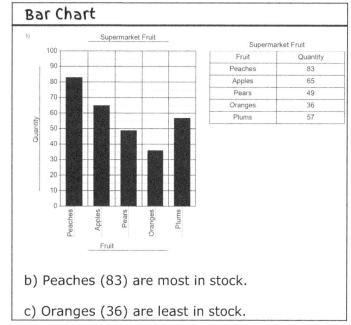

Fruit	Quantity
Peaches	83
Apples	65
Pears	49
Oranges	36
Plums	57

b) Peaches (83) are most in stock.

c) Oranges (36) are least in stock.

Made in the USA
Monee, IL
27 June 2021